Worth Repeating

Giving Children A Second Chance At School Success

by Jim Grant

Published by
Modern Learning Press/
Programs For Education
Rosemont, NJ

10 9 8 7 6 5 4 3 2 1
ISBN 0-935493-21-2

Note: Throughout the book I've used the pronouns he and she interchangeably. In no way have I intended to indicate an imbalance between the sexes.

Dedication

This book is dedicated to my Big Brother, John, who started school in September of 1946 and was assigned to a large first grade class. As a developmentally young, left-handed male who was made to sit on his left hand and forced to write with his right, he was predestined to repeat a grade. In spite of overwhelming odds, he went on to enjoy a very productive life.

Acknowledgments

I would like to thank the following people for their inspiration, encouragement, and commitment to communicate the message that will give children a chance to succeed in life:

My wife Lillian, Cynthia Smith, Linda Skladal and a big thank you to Joanna Foster, a very special editor.

Contents

Worth Repeating

Giving Children A Second Chance At School Success

by Jim Grant

Retention Bill Of Rights

1. Every child has the right to be in the correct grade.
2. Every child has the right, if originally placed in the wrong grade, to be re-placed.
3. Every child has the right to be free of blame if that child needs to be re-placed.
4. Every child has the right to be free from discrimination if re-placed.
5. Every child has the right to be protected from the teasing and torment of other children.
6. Every child has the right to be included in the decision about re-placement.
7. Every child has the right to have school records reflect the fact that the child took two years to complete a grade rather than the indication that the child flunked a grade.
8. Every child has the right to be re-placed at any age or grade at any time during the year.
9. Every child has the right to be taught by teachers who are trained in developmental education.
10. Every child has the right to experience success in learning at school.

CHAPTER 1
Retention And "Re-placement"

Every child has the right to correct grade placement, the right to be in the grade where he or she will flourish and succeed in the tasks of learning. We all want this. We want our children to be happy and successful in school. We want our children to be in the right grade. But it doesn't always work out that way.

Every day thousands of children experience frustration, stress and misery as they try but fail to accomplish the school work they are given. A great many of these children are simply in the wrong grade. In the correct grade, they would experience school success. Through no fault of their own they are overplaced. They are struggling in a grade for which they are not developmentally ready. By being overplaced, these children are unwittingly set up for a school career of frustration and failure.

We don't do this to our children intentionally. It's a mistake, and an easy mistake to make. The law says if a child is five by a certain date, he or she can come to school. The law doesn't recognize whether the child is ready. It doesn't point out that a child who turns five just before the cutoff date is, in fact, one year younger than the classmate whose birthday comes after the cutoff date. The law doesn't appreciate the fact that in the same kindergarten some children are five-going-on-six while others, the *summer children,* are four-just-turned-five. Nor does the law acknowledge that these *summer children* are six to twelve months younger than their classmates, and that a child does a lot of growing in six to twelve months.

In our society, there is the notion that getting a head start on your competitors gives you an advantage.

In our society, there is the notion that getting a head start on your competitors gives you an advantage—and in many situations it does. But not in starting school. If you are not physically, socially, emotionally, and intellectually quite ready for the particular school situation you're put in, it's not an advantage. Instead of your toe being on the starting line, it's several yards behind it.

For a variety of reasons, many children start school *early,* before they are developmentally ready. So in an average first grade, it is still not unusual to find that a high percentage of children are off to a wrong start. More and more, particularly as curriculum requirements increase, these children are put at risk. Unfortunately they are overplaced and we inadvertently set them up for failure.

If a child is overplaced, that child should—that

child has a right to be—re-placed. All children have the right to expect proper grade placement. I don't think that is asking too much. And yet, thousands of children every year are denied the basic right to be in the grade they are developmentally ready for; where they are able to do the work.

We need to recognize the conditions that are creating failure and change them.

As teachers and parents, our main goal is to prevent school failure. We need to stop it before it begins. We need to recognize the conditions that are creating failure and change them. If a child is in the wrong grade and is experiencing great difficulty, we need to correct this mistake. We correct it by re-placing the overplaced child—by putting the child in the grade where his development will be in sync with the demands of the grade. We certainly owe our developmentally young children this second chance at success. Although this sounds right, maybe even simple, it's not.

Re-placement is often confused with retention, and few things are as hotly contested as the value of retention. Few things can trigger as much emotion in parents and children as the idea of *flunking a grade* and having to *stay back.*

For most people the word *retention* is just a polite word that the principal uses for what happens when a child flunks. It is a word that carries extremely negative images.

Let's look at the history of retention. The system of dividing a child's education into grades began in this country in Massachusetts around 1856. It was a convenient system that made it easy to set up and administer schools that encouraged parents to let their children get an education. It was not designed to match the way children learn and develop because in those days no one studied child development. The way the system worked was that if you didn't complete the work for a particular grade, you failed; you didn't pass into the next grade. You were retained. Your failure, so you were told, was due to the fact that you were dumb or lazy; you hadn't applied yourself. Retention was a punishment for doing something wrong.

Retention was a punishment for doing something wrong.

During the second half of the twentieth century, research revealed a great deal about the brain, about how children develop and learn. As a result, remedial and special education classes were implemented to meet the needs of some children. The more we learned about the psychological components of education, the less we favored retention. Failure tends to breed failure, not success.

More recently, since Sputnik in 1957, there has been the cry that our children aren't getting a "good" education and that we need to get back to basics. We hear: "Raise the standards, give children more work, don't pass them unless they have completed the grade." In response to this, researchers are now proving that retaining children who are failing under these conditions doesn't turn failure around.

Unfortunately, what gets overlooked here are the questions about why children are not finishing their work, why they are having great difficulty with it or why they are not getting a "good" education. The way "staying back" has been, and continues to be handled, is completely ignored.

When we talk about the effectiveness of re-placing an overplaced child, the reasons for re-placement and the way it is handled are critical. One of the toughest issues I faced as a principal was what to do for children who weren't ready.

Re-placement can be a life-giving experience.

Re-placement can arouse all the emotions that are associated with retention—denial, distress, anger, guilt. It can be very painful, especially for the adults involved. But, at the same time, re-placement can be a life-giving experience.

Time and time again, I have seen re-placement liberate a child, giving him the opportunity to discover that he is not a failure. I have seen re-placement give a child the chance to affirm for herself that she is a worthwhile individual who can cope successfully with what life offers. Re-placement is developmental progression, not academic retention.

Re-placement will not work well, however, when the root cause of school problems is something other than overplacement. Re-placement cannot resolve problems that grow from hyperactivity, for example, which is often caused by allergies. It will not resolve problems that stem from poor vision or from a learning disability. Re-placement doesn't resolve serious emotional or behavior problems.

In my first book, *I HATE SCHOOL,* which is

about school readiness and developmental placement, I stated, "I firmly believe in re-placing students at any grade level, at any age, at any time during the school year. But it has to be the right child and in the right way. Re-placement is powerful medicine and it must be dispensed with great care." I cannot stress this enough!

Re-placement is powerful medicine and it must be dispensed with great care.

In this book, I discuss how to use re-placement effectively. I look at the children who will benefit from it, how it must be handled, and the alternatives available in our present educational system.

In the following chapters I will share some of my experiences as a teacher and administrator. I will include the advice, suggestions and wisdom of the thousands of teachers nationwide who have freely shared their experiences of children who were overplaced. They affirm over and over again that grade re-placement can be an important and very positive intervention. It can save a child from years of failure and frustration.

CHAPTER 2
Worth Repeating— Success And Re-placement

If you re-place a child and put the child back into sync with the curriculum where the demands match her developmental age, you can, in fact, turn school failure into school success. In this case re-placement is correcting a grade placement that was incorrect in the first place.

Re-placement can resolve the problem of overplacement. If, on the other hand, a child is held back, retained as a consequence of not finishing the curriculum of a particular grade, it will not work. Remember, re-placement is developmental progression, not academic retention.

Re-placement often helps children who are underachieving because they are overplaced. But all underachievers are not necessarily overplaced children. For instance, a child might need to learn at a slower rate due to lower intellectual capacity. Re-placement will not work here. It will not make that child learn faster or increase his IQ. The same holds true with learning disabilities that demand special attention: re-placement without special help is futile and counterproductive. Re-placement will not resolve serious emotional, social or physical problems that might be impeding a child's ability to learn.

Success Is Just Out Of Reach

When we speak of an overplaced child, we mean a child who is immature or too young for a grade. Often these terms, *overplaced* and *immature,* seem to imply that there is something wrong with the child.

Quite the contrary! These young children are developing in a perfectly normal fashion. The only thing *wrong* is that they are in the wrong grade. They are ahead of themselves and are not working from a developmentally strong position. It is as if they are reaching to turn a door knob with their fingertips before they get close enough to get a good grip.

There is a wide range of development among six-year-olds who enter first grade and it is reflected in their skills. Although they all celebrate their sixth birthday in terms of chronological age, developmentally some children are a *strong six,* others are a *strong five-and-a-half,* while others are a *strong five.* Most first grade curricula require the developmental skills of a *strong six* to handle them comfortably. The *strong five* child would be a crackerjack in kindergarten or a pre-first grade program, but in first grade this developmentally young six-year-old would be reaching and struggling and beginning a pattern of stress.

Cognitive, intellectual skills are so important in school that it is easy to forget that it is not just the child's mind that goes to school. The child's physical, emotional and social parts go too, all wrapped up in one person. It is the whole child, with all of these aspects working together, who determines how successful the school experience will be.

If school is frustrating and unrewarding, it will create stress that is reflected in how children act.

PROFILE OF THE OVERPLACED CHILD

Children tell us when they are overplaced and not ready for a particular grade. "I hate school!" is a familiar cry. Or they might express it through behavior that speaks loud and clear. The way children function in school and, interestingly enough, at home, gives us clues that they might be overplaced. There is a sudden change in these children. If school is frustrating and unrewarding, it will create stress that is reflected in their actions.

Matthew Crane, for example, started school when he was not quite five. His birthday wasn't until September 19. Matt started kindergarten when he was still four, because his birthday came before the school system's cutoff date of October 1. Mr. and Mrs. Crane were pleased that their son had made the cutoff date and scored well on the cognitive exam administered to all incoming kindergarten students. They were proud of their boy, and he was excited about starting school.

On the first day of class, Matt clung to his mother when she started to leave. But with a lot of coaxing, he was finally persuaded to stay. By the middle of the first week of kindergarten, he began to cry and have stomach aches in the morning. Getting him off to school was a battle.

Matt's father and mother started pressuring him to go to school, believing they knew what was best. They thought he would "grow out" of this problem. At the end of September they were called to a conference with Matt's teacher.

"Matt is capable of doing the work," Miss Watkins, the kindergarten teacher, said, "but he doesn't concentrate. Instead, he wanders around the room bothering the other children. When I compare Matt to many of his classmates, he seems very young. All he wants to do is play."

Mr. and Mrs. Crane were concerned. In the short time since Matt had started school, their enthusiastic and well-adjusted child had turned into a tense and tired complainer.

"Matt is exhausted when he gets home," his mother told Miss Watkins. "He picks on his youngest sister because he's jealous that she can stay home. He complains all the time about school. He's having nighttime *accidents* again after staying dry for two years. The pediatrician said the problem will go away once Matt gets used to school, but it hasn't. What can we do?"

Miss Watkins made three recommendations: 1. Matt's parents move their child back to pre-kindergarten; 2. allow him to spend two years in kindergarten; 3. keep him with his peers but have the teacher *adjust* the demands on Matt.

Matt's parents opted for the third alternative, which seemed at first to be the right decision. At home, Matt stopped picking on his sister, stopped wetting the bed, and started sharing stories about school. At school, he completed some of his work, but more important to him, he found a friend—someone he could swap food with at snack time and play with at recess. But when it came time to sit at his table, Matt always began to fidget, wanting to sharpen pencils or go to the bathroom or talk to his friend.

In the spring, Miss Watkins told his parents that Matt should be *protected* from first-grade demands. She warned that if Matt were pushed ahead, he might have to repeat a grade at a later age. The Cranes decided to risk it. They wanted to believe their son had made sufficient gains. Matt's *graduation* from kindergarten was cause for rejoicing. Matt had made it! But not for long.

Signs Of Overplacement In Kindergarten

What are the signs that a child like Matt is overplaced in kindergarten?

1) The child's behavior in school seems young and immature in comparison with his classmates. His *fall* birthday is a possible clue to why. He is chronologically as much as eleven months younger than at least two-thirds of the children in the class. But a birthday is not always an indicator that a child will be immature.

2) Though a child is intelligent and does well on a cognitive test, the child has a short attention span and is easily distracted.

3) The child is physically young. Since he hasn't fully developed control over large muscles, he hasn't yet mastered such things as skipping, hopping and catching a ball. Similarly with small muscles, the child is clumsy with crayons or scissors. The child's eye-hand coordination is also developing and is not yet at a point where such

kindergarten tasks as copying letters or numbers is easy.

4) A child like Matt might also be socially and emotionally young and find it hard to get along with other children.

Being developmentally young for a grade puts extra stress on a child. The child expects that because a teacher asks her to do something, she should be able to do it. The child will try and try. But being developmentally young, the task may either be very hard or impossible for the child to do just yet. That can be disappointing, confusing and stressful.

Signs of this stress in kindergarten are:

1) Exhaustion after the school day.

2) Unusual crankiness and disruptiveness at home.

3) Headaches and stomach aches, particularly in the morning.

4) Bed-wetting (especially boys).

The options for the Cranes at the end of kindergarten were to give Matt another year in kindergarten or to let him go into first grade. In some school systems, a third option is available for developmentally young children. There is a pre-first or transition year. Like many parents, the Cranes felt that by having Matt repeat kindergarten they would literally be *holding him back.* He would be bored; he would miss his friends; *he's bright and he'll catch up.*

In September Matt was assigned to an experienced teacher, Ms. Flagg, a veteran of 22 years. Matt's dad told the principal, "We want him with Ms. Flagg. If anyone can make him work, she can." Matt's anxiety level was high as he remembered this same time last year, but he went willingly off to school on the first day.

Because Ms. Flagg knew that Matt needed monitoring, she seated him in the first row. He liked sitting near her desk where he could see the pictures in the book she read every day. What he disliked was sitting near two girls who were nearly a year older than he and who seemed a whole lot smarter. They actually loved school!

First grade became harder and harder for Matt. At home he burst into tears over the least little thing. One evening he confided to his mother that he wasn't as smart as the other children. His mother tenderly assured him that he was very smart. He just needed to *try a little harder*, and soon he would catch up with the rest. Inwardly, Matt's mother sighed. What has happened to this child who had been so quick to learn, so filled with energy and confidence, before he entered school?

Ms. Flagg initiated a conference. "Matthew is certainly intelligent," she said, "but at this stage of his development, he is not ready for the demands of first grade."

Matt's parents were not ready to accept what

Ms. Flagg told them. Surely, they pleaded, if they cooperated with the school, if they worked with Matt at home, if they put him to bed earlier, if they took away his TV privileges, if they were all tougher on him, surely then Matt would succeed. Succumbing to parent pressure, the teacher agreed *to sit on Matt.*

Once again, things were on the upswing—temporarily. Closely monitored and kept under constant pressure, Matt could accomplish average work. He liked receiving extra help, but he knew he wasn't doing as well as expected. Sometimes the harder he tried, the more mistakes he made. That made him feel helpless and stupid. Sometimes he just didn't want to try at all.

In March, Mr. and Mrs. Crane heard exactly what they did not want to hear. Ms. Flagg wanted to retain Matt. She thought his self-concept, already low, might suffer even more if he were promoted and had to spend another year trying to catch up.

Matt's parents were concerned about his self-concept too. "If he's left back, he'll really feel like a failure," his mother said. "He'll miss his friends terribly."

Against Ms. Flagg's recommendation, Matt was promoted on trial. His parents agreed that he would finish first grade over the summer, which made Matt feel cheated. Now he had to spend his vacation doing all that stuff he hated most—math, phonics, and reading. At six years old, life wasn't fair.

Signs Of Overplacement In First Grade

For developmentally young children, it is not a question of catch-up. They are not behind in developing. In fact, they are right on schedule! The only thing out of sync is what we are asking them to do.

In first grade, the teacher might be getting these signs from children who are overplaced:

1) The child complains that the school work is "too hard" and he "can't do it" or that it is "too boring" or even that it is *too easy*, though in fact he doesn't complete it.

2) The child does not shift easily from one task to the next.

3) The child has difficulty adjusting to and completing daily routines.

4) The child experiences difficulty following directions, particularly when asked to do a series of three or four things.

5) The child's attention span is short.

6) The child is straining to keep up, and seeks constant reassurance and praise.

At home, the parents have a child who hates school and continues to show signs of stress—school stomach aches and uncharacteristic behavior.

Within two weeks after the beginning of second grade, Mr. and Mrs. Crane sensed that a storm was brewing. Their son complained, "Ms. Carmen teaches too fast; she never explains things; she doesn't give me enough time."

Early in October, they met with the teacher, whose concerns read like accusations:

> Matt never completes his work.
>
> He doesn't follow instructions.
>
> His verbal self-defense borders on backtalk.
>
> His attention span is very short.
>
> He once tore up a paper in frustration.
>
> He has behaved aggressively toward other children.

Mr. and Mrs. Crane were devastated by this report. Maybe there was something wrong with the school, they thought, or with the teacher—maybe the teacher didn't like Matt. They requested a meeting with the principal, guidance counselor, and teacher, during which all agreed to have Matt tested.

To no one's surprise, the tests proved that Matt's IQ was well above average, though he was six months behind academically. The exam measuring his developmental level showed he was too young for his current grade placement. The principal recommended that Matt take two years in second grade.

Matt's dad replied firmly, "We've made a terrific investment of time and energy in Matt's education. I can't see quitting now. The tests show how intelligent he is. My son is not going to be *held back*—except as a very last resort. Can't you people come up with an acceptable alternative?" Ms. Carmen then devised an individual plan for Matt. Each week the boy signed *a contract* outlining tasks to be done, with rewards and consequences built in. The guidance counselor, Mr. Hall, met with the boy once a week.

To everyone's relief, under this rigid structure, Matt seemed to succeed. At great personal expense, he finished enough of the second grade curriculum to be promoted. Sadly, he brought home his math, phonics, and reading workbooks when school closed for the summer. His schedule allowed little time for play.

SIGNS OF OVERPLACEMENT IN SECOND GRADE

In Second Grade the teacher gets these additional signs of stress from children who are overplaced:

1) The child constantly erases his work.

2) The child has difficulty staying with a task or lesson and is consistently inconsistent about the work.

3) The child cries easily.

4) The child can become either unusually withdrawn, or conversely, unusually aggressive.

5) The child's self-image has suffered over the past two years and the child's low self-esteem is becoming more apparent. Parents too are beginning to see the signs of the child's lack of self-confidence. He is likely to develop a variety of psychosomatic symptoms and expresses a well-founded fear of going into third grade.

On the opening day of school, it was Matt's mother's turn to cry as she watched him go off to school. He had just promised her, "I'm really going to try hard this year. I won't be bad anymore." Forcing Matt to go to school like this just isn't right, Mrs. Crane thought. My boy is really hurting.

Minutes after Matt reached school that morning, he knew he was in deep trouble, as he listened to Mrs. Brennan outline her plans for the year:

"Third graders will learn to tell time to the minute (no digital watches allowed!). You will write with cursive letters...you will make a monthly book report...you will have homework...you will work independently...you must copy accurately from the board."

When Matt came home that day, his mother

took one look at him and knew the whole story. He ran to her in tears, "I will never be able to do all the stupid third grade work! Third grade is dumb." Mrs. Crane held Matt close. I'm always pushing him and pushing him, she thought, and it's just too hard for both of us. Maybe we are making a serious mistake in sending Matt to third grade.

That evening Matt's mother shared her concerns with her husband, but he saw moving his son back a grade as a personal defeat for himself. "Look," he said, "set up an appointment with Mrs. Brennan and we'll see what she has to say about Matt."

When they met with Mrs. Brennan, she was thoroughly familiar with Matt's school history—his situation was well documented. Even so, she believed she could help him *get through* third grade. Reluctantly, Matt's mother agreed with the decision to keep Matt where he was.

Despite everyone's best efforts, Matt fell further and further behind. For his parents, life seemed to drag along from one school conference to the next. They wondered how they had failed their son. They wondered how long they could endure their nightly tussles with homework.

In December Matt's parents were invited to an evening meeting, sponsored by the PTA, on the subject of school success and school failure. There they heard a speaker outlining the concepts of school readiness and proper grade placement, and they listed parents whose children had been left back a grade as they enthusiastically endorsed the idea.

After the conference, Mrs. Crane said firmly, "I know that Matt belongs in second grade."

SIGNS OF OVERPLACEMENT IN THIRD GRADE

In third grade, teachers see these kinds of stress from overplaced children:

1) The child mixes printing and cursive writing unintentionally. Cursive writing is difficult.
2) The child finds it hard to handle the volume of work.
3) The child has a difficult time learning the multiplication tables.
4) The child does not work well independently and can't keep track of pencils, papers or books.
5) The child daydreams much of the time.
6) The child seldom if ever volunteers for routine school activities.
7) The child has difficulty understanding abstractions such as concepts and relationships. Cause and effect are still hard to grasp. The

child is much better with subjects that are concrete.

At home as the child goes into third grade and beyond, parents may likely observe:

1) Their child demands assistance with nightly homework.
2) Their child is preoccupied with fear of being promoted into the next grade.
3) Their child might develop a nervous tic such as a cough or constant clearing of the throat or twirling a strand of hair.
4) Their child prefers to play with younger children.
5) Their child completes school work only under constant pressure.
6) Their child has a poor self-image and low self-esteem.

Matt moved back to second grade where he was able to do the work and the stress was eased. It was not an easy decision for his parents. It was an adjustment for Matt during which the support and encouragement of his parents and teachers were of critical importance. But it gave Matt the opportunity to experience success in school and begin to rebuild his self-image.

There are hundreds of boys and girls like Matt.

Some continue the struggle through all twelve grades. Others, like Matt, falter as they enter third, fourth or fifth grades and the question of retention or *re-placement* comes up. For overplaced children, correcting the placement by re-placing the child is most easily done between kindergarten and third grade. It is never easy on the parents; but the early years are easier on the child. Adjusting to re-placement grows harder as the child grows older. Nevertheless, re-placement is still a viable option for many older children.

THE BENEFITS OF RE-PLACEMENT:

1) Greatly Reduced School-Induced Stress

When a child is re-placed and his developmental age is in sync with the demands of the grade, the stress he was experiencing is greatly relieved. The signs of negative stress that were so evident before—crying easily, hating school, frequent headaches and stomach aches and nervous tics—will disappear.

2) Increased Comfort Level

In the correct grade a child will find a new comfort level. There is a sense of fitting in and no longer being different or at the bottom of the ladder.

3) A Chance Is Provided To Compete Successfully

The child who is asked to perform beyond her

capacity will feel inadequate and inferior. Re-placing a child to where she can perform adequately puts her on an equal footing with her peer group and makes it possible for her to compete on an equal basis.

4) Increased Willingness To Take Risks

The child who struggles or performs poorly soon learns not to take chances. He will participate as little as possible to avoid the possibility of being wrong or of making a mistake. He will distance himself and find ways to become inconspicuous so as not to be called on. He may do the required work but nothing more. In the correct grade he will experience success and being *right,* his willingness to take risks will gradually increase.

5) A Child's Position Is Changed In The Class

Parents of a re-placed child frequently report, "My child was at the bottom of the class last year and would come home crying every day. This year he says school is *cinchy.*" It is common to hear parents say "We have a new child this year." Children know the routine and curriculum the second time around which makes it more comfortable. Since they will have grown physically, they might emerge as the class leader and top athlete.

6) The Child's Self Concept Is Enhanced

School misery and failure are demoralizing. They eat away at a child's natural self-confidence and self-esteem. Re-placement gives the child a chance to distance herself from the humiliation and embarrassment of school failure.

7) Life At Home Improves

School problems always find their way home and create conflict. An unhappy, unsuccessful child becomes a family problem. The frustration and tension spread to the parents and often aggravate a child's relationship with his brothers and sisters. When the stress of school failure is diminished, things at home improve.

8) More Positive Energy For Teacher And Parents

It is demoralizing for the teacher and parents when a child is suffering and not learning. Not being able to help a child is worrisome and frequently heartbreaking. Conversely, being able to help the child on a level where she is able to succeed can be rewarding and invigorating.

CHAPTER 3
Age And Re-placement

"Children run on different developmental timetables. By age six, teachers expect up to two year's difference in maturation among their students. Moreover, each child has a unique profile of strengths and weaknesses—physical, emotional, intellectual, and social. One of the hardest things for everyone to understand is that bright children are not necessarily on the fastest train. Many problems of *underachievement* result from an incongruity between the child's neurological timetable and the expectations of the family and school." *Jane M. Healy, Ph.D. Your Child's Growing Mind*

DEVELOPMENTAL AGE

Our chronological age is set by the calendar. Our developmental age is set by our internal clock. Each of us is born with our own particular internal clock—a pattern and rate of growth that is distinctly our own. It is established by our genes and it stays with us throughout our lives.

These internal clocks don't all keep the same time. For instance, you probably observed a growth pattern when your child began to speak. Most children start to talk between ten and fourteen months, but there are marked differences. If your child began to talk at fifteen to eighteen months that didn't signify a problem. It was a matter of development, a matter of time. School curricula assume a certain level of development in the child's nervous system. Classroom structure demands a certain level of development from a child's eyes and small muscles. To cope with the school environment a child must have a certain level of social and emotional maturity.

If chronological age is the only consideration for starting a child in school, then a child whose development is uneven could be placed at risk. The key factor, then, in a profile of the kind of child who will benefit from grade re-placement, is developmental age.

Developmental age is best determined by a combination of three things: parent's observation of medical and developmental history; teacher's classroom observations; and an individual developmental assessment by a trained examiner.

THE SOONER THE BETTER

The sooner an overplaced child is re-placed and is working at a comfortable, successful level, the better it is. The younger a child is, the easier it is for him to make friends among his new classmates.

Struggling along in school can seriously undermine a child's confidence and self-esteem.

Kindergartners might at first pick up anxious feelings about re-placement from their parents or older children, but once the new year begins and they become comfortable and happy again. The anxiety quickly disappears. This is a good reason why, when children are young, the decision about repeating a grade should rest with parents. And, although it is always important to talk with the child about the decision, the decision itself should not be left to the child.

EXPERIENCING YEARS OF OVERPLACEMENT

Overplaced children can struggle in school and experience difficulty without actually coming to the point of failing. This is particularly true of bright children who are developmentally young.

Struggling in school can seriously undermine a child's confidence and self-esteem. Year after year the struggle also reinforces all the unproductive *survival techniques*: procrastination, avoiding taking risks, avoiding responsibility and similar defensive behavior.

In many cases re-placement can still help the older child. I have known fourth and fifth graders who flourished when they repeated a grade. Teachers, parents and children themselves have told me over and over again of what a godsend it was that they decided or were encouraged to repeat a grade. These are stories about children who were near failure, or marginal performers who suddenly began to experience success. These are stories of kids who got out from under demoralizing stress and pressure and by repeating a grade, developed a sense of self-worth and accomplishment.

It is never too late to correct overplacement. It is never too late to repeat a grade, if doing so will resolve a child's problems. But as a child moves into the upper elementary grades, peer pressure increases, and it is important to evaluate with the young person just what he stands to gain against what he feels he will lose.

Older Children See Themselves As Failures

It is not surprising that research reveals a high correlation between juvenile delinquency and school failure. School failure directly causes over three-quarters of the children to drop out of school. *School failure* isn't just incomplete grades and flunking courses, it is years of frustration and lack of success that cause children to see themselves as dumb, failures, useless or all of these.

This frustration can begin because the child is overplaced and too young for kindergarten or first grade. Once it develops into a long history of school difficulty and failure, then repeating a grade at an older age might not be the right answer. Defensive behavior and a lack of confidence in adult promises that things will improve can block a child's ability to see re-placement as anything but punishment and further *proof* of failure. If a child has become locked into this image of failure, the child needs help of a different kind. The key to success is no longer simply grade re-placement.

Frank was such a child. Frank was born in August, the third of three boys. The family situation was anything but stable. Dad was a long distance truck driver, but alcoholism kept him from holding a steady job. The family had continual financial problems. Despite the family turmoil, Frank was a happy child with a great interest in *the world*. He wore his mother out always asking *why*.

Frank was crushed when all his friends went to nursery school and he couldn't go, because his family couldn't afford it. The next year, they couldn't afford to send him to a private kindergarten program and the school didn't have a publicly funded kindergarten. Frank first attended school in first grade without the advantage of having attended either nursery school or kindergarten.

When the time came for Frank to go to school,

he wondered how it would be. His two older brothers failed first grade and he constantly heard his parents complain about the school, and especially the teachers.

Frank's mother wondered too. When she enrolled him in first grade, she expressed her fear that he seemed too young to cope with the demands of first grade. She remembered the struggle of her other two boys. They tried to do well in school but failed and were forced to repeat. Both boys were still doing marginal work at best.

In mid-September, at the first of many teacher conferences, her worst fears came true. The teacher expressed concern that Frank was unable to stay on task and focus on his school work. His short attention span handicapped him in every activity. Frank seemed anxious much of the time and the stress was causing him to have temper outbursts. He frequently cried and complained that the work was too hard and besides it was *dumb*.

His mother told the teacher that Frank had reverted to bed wetting and didn't like school anymore. He agreed to stay at home and help out around the house. Things were just not going well in Frank's world.

The teacher felt that the best thing for Frank would be to give him two years to finish the first-year program. Frank's mother tentatively agreed. When she brought up the subject with her husband, he flatly said "No! Our other sons failed and repeated. It didn't do them much good. We are not going to have the same thing happen to Frank!" In the end his parents insisted he go on to second grade.

Struggling in the wrong grade only increased the pressure on Frank. It seemed like the harder he tried, the further behind he got. By Christmas vacation, he was stressed to the limit and exhibiting serious behavior problems. Even with tutoring, he still felt stupid. He worried constantly about catching up to his classmates.

Frank's parents blamed the school for not giving him enough attention and extra help. They didn't like or have confidence in his teacher—or so it seemed to Frank. He was well aware of the tension between his parents and the school.

In June, it was recommended that Frank take two years to complete second grade. The teacher expressed concern that Frank was not only far behind in his work but that he was so young socially and emotionally that he would have great difficulty in coping with the demands of the next grade.

Again, Frank's father was adamant that he not stay back. Frank's misery in school continued, and predictably each year was marked by low achievement and poor test scores, behavior problems, and a shaky self-concept.

During sixth grade, Frank's parents divorced and his father moved away. In talking to Frank's mother, the sixth grade teacher suggested once again that Frank repeat the grade as a chance to *catch up* before changing buildings and going to Junior High. Frank protested. He hated the idea. But his mother agreed, thinking it was the best thing for him.

For Frank, repeating sixth grade was the crowning blow. What friends he had were gone. He was humiliated and felt like a complete failure. His self-esteem hit an all-time low. He cut school whenever he could and dreamed of the day when he would be old enough to quit school forever.

His behavior, both at home and at school, grew worse. He was frequently tardy and was absent 65 days. His mother was worn out battling him each morning to go to school, and at night to do his homework. Repeating the grade hadn't made matters any better. In fact, she felt things were getting worse.

By sixth grade, Frank was a poor candidate for re-placement for several reasons:

1) From the start his parents saw re-placement as failure. Their first two sons had failed and they felt that re-placing Frank in the first grade would be a third failure. They thought Frank and the school were at fault. By blaming the school, they undermined Frank's confidence in school. He questioned if the school cared whether he learned or not.

2) Family and emotional distractions

interfered with learning. There was little family encouragement and support to free Frank to concentrate on school work.

3) A child who has experienced a history of failure with a particular curriculum will show little progress simply repeating the same material.

4) Frank's poor self-concept weakened his spirit and undermined his confidence and ability to work hard. Frank felt threatened and defeated by retention. He had no grounds to see it as an opportunity.

5) Frank's behavior problems had become habitual. Some were serious enough to stand in the way of his learning.

Behavior Problems And Overplacement

Frank started school as an overplaced child, too young for first grade. His inappropriate behavior, to a large degree, was a response to this. Re-placement, however, would have been hard for him because his parents didn't understand the need for it. In fact, they were against it. If they had supported it, there is every probability that his inappropriate behavior would have disappeared. As it happened, Frank's behavior—triggered by over-placement in the first place—was reinforced to the point where it became habitual. Increasingly, it became apparent that re-placement alone could not longer solve the problem.

Re-placement means a big change for children. How you approach them about this idea is critical.

Believing Re-placement Is Worth A Try

Re-placement means a big change for children. How you approach them about this idea is critical. If they are willing to give it a try...if they believe that it really might make life better...if the risks don't seem too great, then re-placement has a very good chance of working.

Parents, child and teacher should be involved in the decision-making process. It is best if everyone is open and supportive of one another during this time. After this process, especially with younger children (those in kindergarten and first grade), the parents always make the final decision. With older children, on the other hand, it is important to let the child have a say in the decision.

Just as an administrator would be unwise to re-place a child against the parents' wishes, it would be unwise to re-place an older child who is dead set against re-placement. Whatever short-term improvement might be gained is at the risk of the child feeling helpless and resentful in the long run. These feelings will seriously hamper the child's ability to become involved in resolving his school problem.

BOREDOM

Very bright overplaced children might feel uncomfortable socially and emotionally.

Children with average or above average intelligence are among those who benefit most from re-placement. You often hear people say that these children could do better if only they tried. These children don't necessarily fail, but because they are developmentally young, they are not able to harness and use their full potential.

Very bright overplaced children might feel uncomfortable socially and emotionally. They are often happier playing with younger children. Many adults are concerned that a bright, developmentally young child might be bored if re-placed. I have never witnessed this. What I have noticed is that these children, because their social, emotional, and physical development comes into sync with what is required of them, grow. They become interested and not bored. As these facets develop, they support and encourage the child to use her intellectual abilities.

PHYSICAL SIZE

In grade re-placement being small is helpful, but being large also has some advantages. It makes sense that children who are small for their chronological age would adapt more readily to re-placement. They blend in with the younger children. Fitting in and being accepted makes a child feel comfortable and builds self-confidence.

It is the child's developmental age that is thought to have the greatest impact on school success.

There are no hard and fast rules, however, about the relationship between physical size and grade placement. School readiness and maturity are not measured by pounds and inches but by developmental age. It is the child's developmental age that is thought to have the greatest impact on school success.

Some children who are re-placed will be almost a year older than their youngest classmate, chronologically. If this child happens to be large for his age, the dynamics dramatically change. If a child is especially sensitive about being larger or more developed physically, the adjustment to the new peer group could be difficult.

Still, there are some advantages in being larger. Larger children often excel in sports. With self-confidence, they may also be looked up to as leaders.

Because skill in sports such as football and baseball improves with size and physical maturity, there are, in some parts of the country, age restrictions in senior high school sports. Children who are re-placed might run into these. Disappointing? Yes.

A reason to keep a child struggling in the wrong grade? I don't think so.

Illness Or Accident

When a child misses a significant amount of school work due to a serious illness or accident it is logical to suggest grade re-placement. It is also far easier for parents and child to understand and accept re-placement under these conditions.

Decide on grade re-placement only after determining that it seems the best of all the options for the particular child.

As with all decisions, it is important to consider all options and include the child in the decision-making process. If the child had been happy and doing well in school, you might question whether she would be able to make up the work with tutoring or in summer school. Or perhaps she would be able to keep up with the work while in the hospital or at home. Decide on grade re-placement only after determining that it seems the best of all the options for the particular child.

CHAPTER 4
Children Who Need More Than Re-placement

"Very seldom is there any substantial special help provided to repeating pupils; instead they are recycled through a program that was inappropriate for them the first time around." —*Gregg B. Jackson. The Research Evidence On The Effect Of Grade Retention*

For overplaced children, grade re-placement can make all the difference in the world. It can be a life-saver. It is a powerful and effective remedy for their *problem,* which is being in the wrong grade.

But as with all powerful remedies, re-placement is not the cureall for every child with school difficulties. If a child has a neurologically based learning disability, he needs an educational program that helps him compensate for that disability. If a child is a slow learner, she needs instruction that is designed to help slow learners develop to their full potential. If a child has serious behavioral problems, he needs a careful diagnosis of what is triggering the unacceptable behavior and, possibly, to get professional help. This is also true of children with emotional problems.

These children do not need re-placement; they need programs that will meet their special needs. Will re-placement hurt these children? Only if it is used in place of the help they really need. If a child with a special need is re-placed—and such a child could also be developmentally immature—there could be short-term improvement but the problem would not be resolved.

To learn, a child needs to feel good about himself.

To learn, a child needs to feel good about himself. Later in this book, I will talk about how critical it is for the child to understand why he is being re-placed and how he can make things better. You see, if a child fails and has no idea why or no reason to think things can get better, retention is "proof" of failure. If a child doesn't believe that in some way he can succeed in school, retention is only going to compound his alienation from the educational system. Research shows that among high school students who drop out, over 75 percent had failed and had been retained one or more times. In this case, the retention caused by years of school failure is not re-placement, but academic retention.

Faced with this kind of research and statistics, some educators have opted to avoid retention at all cost. Pass everyone and then no one will feel like a failure. Such a blanket policy doesn't work. When you pass overplaced children who need re-placement, you lock them into a pattern of stress that denies them success. As I said, repeating a grade is not the answer for every child, but this is not a valid reason for denying re-placement to those who will benefit from it. Or as they say in Vermont: just because the roof leaks, don't tear the house down. The key, of course, is matching the right remedy with the right children—those whose problems stem from overplacement.

Children With Learning Disabilities

It is difficult to identify neurologically based learning disabilities at an early age. Take a child like Wayne.

Wayne's mom was very aware of her child's clumsiness as a preschooler and his frustration when he tried to learn new things. He seemed eager to go to nursery school when he was four, but his eagerness was dampened on the first day. He found it very difficult to follow directions and work in a play group.

He fought so hard against going to nursery school that his mother gave up and kept him home. Since he loved being at home and having one friend over to play with, Mom felt the year at home was just what he needed to grow. She did, however, worry that he seemed to have more difficulty learning than other children.

When Wayne started kindergarten, it was a traumatic experience. He liked recess, singing, play time, and lunch, but he didn't like learning numbers and letters because they got too *mixed up.* Nor did he enjoy games that required a lot of directions.

Wayne's kindergarten teacher was wonderful. She really understood him and was quick to help him find ways to do his work. Early in the school year, however, she began to suspect he had some form of learning handicap. She recommended testing and evaluation, but was refused because the school officials felt that testing would not be valid on a child Wayne's age. Evaluation would have to wait two more years.

He was promoted to first grade under the condition that his next teacher monitor his progress closely.

Except for *dumb old reading* and having to follow so many orders, Wayne said he liked first grade. Unfortunately, he continued to experience great difficulty doing any work related to reading and writing. He constantly reversed, inverted or substituted his letters. By the end of first grade, he was barely reading, which was insufficient for the demands of second grade.

His teacher recommended that Wayne's parents re-place him in first grade to see if another year would help. She felt second grade would be too frustrating this year, but by next year he'd be better prepared. If he hadn't made sufficient progress by spring of next year, she suggested that he undergo a full psycho-educational evaluation to determine an appropriate course of action.

At the end of his second year in first grade, Wayne made minimal progress. Although he had a comfortable year, it did nothing to change his learning problems. When evaluation results showed that Wayne had a learning disability, it came as no surprise to anyone.

Repeating a year will not change a child's neurologically-based learning disability.

Wayne's parents were both relieved and distraught. Finally the puzzle was solved. Now Wayne would get the help he so desperately needed. On one hand, they felt fortunate because their school had excellent special services so Wayne would at last receive help. On the other hand they were upset because it had taken three full years to conclude that their child needed special help. What was the reason for waiting so long? They felt a valuable year had been wasted by repeating when it proved such a negligible gain.

Wayne was done a disservice. What he really needed in the beginning was a full evaluation followed by an Individual Education Plan (IEP). The IEP would outline the particular special services that would meet Wayne's needs.

With Wayne the problem was not developmental youngness; it was not in his best interest to delay the necessary services. If Wayne had been both developmentally young and learning disabled, the repeated year would have been helpful, provided that an IEP had been developed and he was getting the special help he needed.

Wayne's parents were justified in questioning the re-placement year, because research clearly shows that repeating a year will not change a child's neurologically-based learning disability.

Overplaced And Learning Disabled

Many overplaced children have been tagged learning disabled.

In pre-school, kindergarten and even first grade, the behavior of an overplaced child and a learning disabled child will bear a close similarity. Both are marked by signs of immaturity. Both may exhibit an intelligence that outstrips their ability to function in the particular grade.

Because of this similarity, many overplaced children have been tagged learning disabled. Luckily this is changing as we discover more about learning disabilities, but there is still a long way to go. Therefore, it is important that the concept of learning disabilities not be a catchall for both neurological learning disabilities and learning difficulties whose cause lies elsewhere.

The overplaced child's apparent immaturity will *disappear* when her developmental age is in sync with the grade level and curriculum. What makes the learning disabled child different is, as Sally Smith explains in *No Easy Answers*, "the quantity, intensity and long duration of immature behavior."

In *Questions Parents Ask: Straight Answers From Louise Bates Ames*, Dr. Ames lists clues that indicate a possible learning disability in the school-age child. Dr. Alan C. Levin, who developed these clues, cautions that any child might exhibit one or even several signs. A true learning disability is suspect only if parents answer yes to more than ten of these questions (which is 20 per cent).

1. Does your child have difficulty understanding what he reads?
2. Does he avoid sports or activities that involve catching or throwing a ball?
3. Is your child afraid of heights?
4. Is he extremely daring?
5. Does his running seem to you uncoordinated and sloppy?
6. Does he get lost frequently?
7. Is he easily distracted?
8. Does he confuse right and left?
9. Does he use one hand for some things and the other hand for other things?
10. Is he up and down from the table at mealtime?
11. Is he a discipline problem?
12. Does he go up and down stairs one step at a time?
13. Does he seem bright and articulate but seem not to understand what he reads?
14. Is he the class clown?
15. Do people say he is not working up to potential?

16. Does he seem to *tune out* at times?
17. Is he unusually forgetful?
18. Does he find it necessary to touch everything?
19. Does he walk into things or trip?
20. Is his behavior inconsistent?
21. Does he have a short attention span?
22. Does he move his lips while reading or follow the line with his fingers?
23. Does he have frequent headaches?
24. Is he purposely destructive?
25. Does he frustrate easily?
26. Is he unusually sensitive to light, noise, touch?
27. Was he a late walker?
28. Was he a prolonged tiptoe walker?
29. Was his speech late or abnormal?
30. Is he a bed-wetter?
31. Does he have uncontrollable rages?
32. Does he complain of seeing things bigger or smaller than they actually are?
33. Does he find it hard to keep up with other children?
34. Does he have a poor appetite?
35. Does he have a history of allergies?

36. Is he irritable before or shortly after mealtime?
37. Does he crave sweets?
38. Has he ever experienced excessive weight loss or gain?
39. Does he go outside the lines when coloring?
40. Did he have trouble learning how to tie or button or lace?
41. Was he colicky?
42. Was he a cranky baby?
43. Was he an unusually passive baby?
44. Is he a bully?
45. Is he always picked on by classmates?
46. Is he a loner?
47. Does he seek out older or younger playmates?
48. Does his play seem to you clumsy or disjointed?
49. When he reads out loud, does he get mixed up and lose his place?
50. Does he not complete homework assignments?

The Slow Learner

Experts generally agree that children with low ability show minimal gains when they are re-placed. In fact, they may actually be worse off. A slow learner will usually show greater gains with alternatives to re-placement such as remedial work or direct instruction. Betty was such a child.

Betty had a fairly happy pre-school experience. Kindergarten started out okay too though her nursery school teacher thought she might be overwhelmed. By November, however, she was beginning to fall apart. Her mother was aware of Betty's growing frustration.

In school, Betty was a quiet, compliant child who learned to cooperate and not get *noticed*. It is typical for this kind of child to go through the motions and survive at school, but once at home, to fall apart and frequently end the afternoon in tears. Usually this happens because the child cannot keep up with the pace of the class.

When Betty's Mom told the teacher about what was happening at home, the teacher was able to alleviate some of the pressure Betty was feeling. She started by giving Betty much more individualized attention. As long as the teacher worked with her on a one-to-one basis, Betty was able to do most of the work. Unfortunately at year's end, even with special attention, Betty had not made as much progress as expected. Since she processed information at a very slow rate, her work was painfully slow. Besides that, her attention span was very short and her memory, both short-and long-term, was not strong.

One option was to re-place Betty in kindergarten to give her more time with the kindergarten curriculum. Another consideration was to have her evaluated for possible learning disabilities. It was pointed out that although evaluations at this early age might not be definitive, testing could indicate areas of potential difficulty. In Betty's case the evaluation produced no signs of disability, but the general level of her ability to learn came into question.

Slow learners, those with less than average ability, do not do as well, and in some cases do worse the second time in the same grade.

Being a slow learner with below-average intelligence, Betty's difficulty in school made sense. Of course she would get lost in group instruction and yet function in a one-to-one tutoring situation. She needed to be in a small group with plenty of individualized instruction.

Rather than re-placing Betty in kindergarten, her parents and the school agreed that she should go on into a special first grade program designed to meet the needs of low-ability children.

There is a substantial body of research that indicates slow learners, those with less than average ability, do not do as well, and in some cases, do worse the second time in the same grade.

A report published in 1981 by the Educational Research Information Center stated that research clearly reveals that "neither retention nor promotion by itself solves the problems of low-achieving students...who continue to perform below class average."

Group IQ tests are usually not reliable when the question of ability is a factor in re-placement. For a decision of this magnitude, the child should be given an individual IQ test. Equally important, the test results should be corroborated by both the parents and the teacher's observations. Personal observations are extremely important. There is a high correlation between these observations and the test results.

Re-placement does not address the cause of behavioral problems; therefore, it cannot resolve them.

SERIOUS BEHAVIOR PROBLEMS

If a child is prone to outbursts, has an unusually high activity level, and is unable to pay attention or respond to direction, this child tempts school failure. She risks falling behind not only academically, but socially as well because there is a natural tendency for children to ostracize anyone demonstrating belligerent or antisocial behavior. Having no one to play with only compounds the problem.

How can these children be promoted if they fall behind and don't complete their work by the end of the year? It would seem that re-placement is the answer. But it isn't.

Re-placement does not address the cause of behavioral problems; therefore, it cannot resolve them. It can, in fact, aggravate them. Take for instance, anti-social behavior developed as a defense against a shaky sense of self-worth. In this case, re-placement is a blow to the child and can cause even more defensive behavior. These children need realistic, practical solutions that address the causes of the behavior.

Advances in child psychology have enabled parents and educators to better understand what triggers different kinds of unacceptable behavior. It might be a defense mechanism prompted by a move, death, divorce, alcoholism, child abuse, or some other form of turmoil in the home. There are also many less dramatic causes such as the pressure of inappropriate expectations from home, school and society. Unacceptable behavior can be triggered by things in the child's environment like chemicals, fumes or odors. It may also be traced to allergies or hypersensitivity to certain foods and medicines.

In his book *Superimmunity For Kids,* Dr. Leo Galland writes: "In my practice I have treated many difficult children, and I've found that with nutritional treatment, the personalities of difficult preschoolers often change amazingly for the better. Once a child is over seven years old, though, and patterns of aggressive, manipulative, or self-destructive behavior are well established, nutritional treatment may no longer be enough."

Dr. Galland writes at length about the kinds of problems that arise from allergies and biochemical hypersensitivity. He discusses how to discover the possible causes and how to treat them nutritionally.

A child who is difficult and behaves badly creates an unhappy situation for all, but most importantly for himself. His attitudes and actions produce negative feedback that, in turn, can make his behavior worse. He develops a poor self-image that is likely to be reinforced in school by teachers and classmates who find him hard to handle.

By looking for the cause of inappropriate behavior, changes can be made that produce long-term results.

By looking for the cause of inappropriate behavior, changes can be made that produce long-term results. School counselors are a wonderful resource in this area. They often work with teachers, parents and child to bring about change through behavior modification techniques. More resources for helping children change inappropriate behavior patterns are listed in the bibliography. Be sure to note Dr. Stanley Turecki, *The Difficult Child,* and *Questions Parents Ask: Straight Answers From Louise Bates Ames,* in particular.

CHAPTER 5
Stress, Self-esteem, And Re-placement

"Teachers viewed the self-concept of non-promoted children as either stable or becoming more positive in 96 percent of the cases during the repeated school year... An overwhelming majority (79.2 percent) of parents viewed their non-promoted child as being more confident and successful in school during the repeated school year than the year before." *H. J. Finlayson, Phi Delta Kappan*

THE PURPOSE IS TO RELIEVE STRESS

For generations there was one cause for repeating a grade apart from illness: you flunked. You failed and had to repeat. Better luck next time.

While many parents (and most grandparents) still believe this, there is a growing number of parents who understand that re-placement is not a sign of failure, doom or gloom. In fact, some younger parents were re-placed in kindergarten and first grade themselves and can now validate the positive experience. Still, many parents have a hard time seeing re-placement as anything but failure. So again and again the question comes up: Won't there be a stigma attached to repeating a grade?

Won't there be a stigma attached to repeating a grade?

Usually the question is approached in terms of the child feeling stigmatized. Interestingly enough, stigma is something adults feel and are concerned about far more than children. But, ideas are contagious and if parents and siblings believe that re-placement means failure, it's only a matter of time before the child believes it as well.

What a child believes is important. A child enters school having had only five short years to develop some sense of who he is and what he can do. The primary school years are a critical time for developing a self-image. If a young child can't do something that a teacher expects him to do, or that other children can do, he feels it is his fault. Young children haven't developed defenses to protect their self-esteem, as adults have. For instance, if we get poor instructions for assembling a do-it-yourself project, we fault the instructions, not ourselves. If we read an obtuse, confusing book, we don't question our ability to read, but the author's ability to write. An overplaced first grader, on the other hand, is not able to tell herself: "The reason this primer is impossible to read is that it has been given to me too soon. The teacher has made a mistake and given me something that is developmentally inappropriate."

While adults defend their self-esteem against mistakes or failings that aren't their fault, children feel responsible for them. When a child is expected to read a book or do a math problem and can't, he feels it must be his fault. There must be something he did wrong or, if frustrated again and again, something wrong with him. Young children are still largely defenseless in their emotional development and very vulnerable with regard to their self-image.

While adults defend their self-esteem against mistakes or failings that aren't their fault, children feel responsible for theirs.

Throughout life, we are continually defining who we are, asking ourselves questions like:

What is Self-Esteem?

Am I good or bad?

Do I count for something?

Can I learn to do things?

Am I as good as other people?

We measure ourselves in terms of our acceptance by others and our achievements. And the result is what we think of ourselves—our self-esteem. It is an ongoing process, and the feedback isn't always positive. But a healthy self-esteem, built on a foundation of positive experiences, gives us the strength to learn from mistakes and failures. People who talk about turning failure into success, believe in themselves. They know they can learn. They know they can cope. They have a healthy self-esteem and a good self-image.

The reason for re-placement, the reason for

developmentally young children repeating a grade, is to give them the opportunity to develop a good self-image, a healthy self-esteem in order to enjoy learning.

It is the child's attitudes and beliefs that power the performance cycle of learning.

There is a pattern to learning. Martin L. Seldman, in his book *Performance Without Pressure*, calls it the "The Performance Cycle." At the top of this cycle we find a child's attitudes and beliefs about herself and what is to be learned. From these attitudes spring feelings and motivation. These lead to making an effort. And, of course, from the effort comes a result. But it doesn't end there. The result feeds directly back into what a child believes about herself. It is the child's attitudes and beliefs that power this performance cycle of learning.

Arthur R. Jensen points out in *Understanding Readiness: An Occasional Paper* that "The child's own perception of his increasing mastery of the skill to be acquired is the most effective reinforcement of learning. When this perception is lacking, learning bogs down."

Emotions Play A Big Part

According to Paul MacLean, director of the Laboratory of Brain Evolution and Behavior at the National Institute of Mental Health, "We try to be rational, intellectual, to be wary of our emotions, but the only part of the brain that can tell us what we perceive to be real things is the limbic brain."

The limbic part of the brain controls our emotional responses. It sits in the middle between the part that controls our deepest, most instinctive behavior and the rational part that controls abstract thinking necessary for reading, writing and math. So perceiving, feeling and thinking are interconnected.

Perceiving, feeling and thinking are interconnected.

Look at what happens when a child is having trouble learning. Day by day the overplaced child experiences disappointment, frustration and the humiliation of not being able to perform up to what's expected of him. This builds up emotional stress, so the child's energy is pulled away from the rational part of the brain and focuses on the emotional part. The overplaced child who is already having a hard time with the curriculum is now tying up an increasing amount of energy on an emotional level that would better serve him on a rational level. A child who is immature and over his head in kindergarten or first grade is basically confused by why things are not going well in school. She tries to make sense of why she's not able to do what is expected. She may grow to feel that she is letting her parents down or disappointing the teacher.

The child begins to feel that he can't do the work and is not as good as the others. A child like this may often feel left out, picked on or like the low man on the totem pole. Then the question arises, "Is there something wrong with me?"

As the stress continues unabated, it grows into distress. "Why do it? Why bother, I can't do the work anyway." Any sense of challenge has turned into hopelessness. Distress is debilitating and it impedes the child's ability to function.

Some overplaced children struggle along performing marginally but never up to their potential. Others give up hope, cease to try and spiral into dysfunction. Either way, dysfunction *proves* to the child that he or she is not a capable person. Inadequacy has been miserably proven out.

Even if the overplaced child manages to struggle along through the grades, she pays a heavy price in self-esteem.

Even if the overplaced child manages to struggle along through the grades, she pays a heavy price in self-esteem. The purpose of re-placement is to relieve the stress, to release the emotional energy and to put children in a learning situation where they can rebuild their self-esteem.

If Self-esteem Will Not Be Improved, Don't Re-place

When re-placement does not help to rebuild a child's self-esteem, it tends to do just the opposite. Re-placement works when it resolves the problem of an eroding self-esteem. It works easily in kindergarten, before the stress has begun to take its toll. It works well in first and second grade, with special attention from parents and teachers to help the child rebuild a positive self-image. It can work in third, fourth and fifth grade. It can work in even higher grades. But as the overplaced child grows older, the need to work with the child in terms of self-image becomes more complex and more critical. This is why, with an older child, it is essential that the child be willing to give re-placement a try. Kindergarten children, on the other hand, are usually satisfied with a careful explanation.

Re-placement can be a positive experience because it is a second chance at success. With your help, your child will realize this second chance.

Re-placement can be a positive experience because it is a second chance at success.

CHAPTER 6

Today's Positive Options—Kindergarten Through Second Grade

As we learn more and more about child development, an increasing number of school systems are beginning to see the value of determining developmental readiness for school together with providing a flexible program to accommodate the needs of young children. Although these programs go by different names, all are designed to give developmentally young children the extra time they need to begin a successful school career. These transition programs are called pre-Kindergarten or young fives, pre-first, junior first, readiness class or primary I and transition second or primary II.

The curriculum in these programs is not remedial; it is developmental. "We see this distinction as crucial," write educators Gerald Jennings, Jacqueline Lohraff and Jane Rizzo in their article "Retention: A Positive Alternative." They go on to explain, "A remedial program is based on the premise that the student should have learned and didn't—so remediation is necessary. A developmental program is based on the premise that the student has not yet learned—so the program meets the children at their current level of development and provides appropriate instruction. Remedial programs go over the materials again. Developmental programs start at the point where success can be experienced and then move forward....

Developmental programs start at the point where success can be experienced and then move forward.

"Although we don't expect children to have more than one such experience during their stay at our school, we anticipate that as many as 50 percent could take four years to complete an education that traditionally requires three years. [k-2]"

READY OR NOT HERE I COME!

Summer Children, Ready Or Not For School, by James K. Uphoff, Ph.D., June Gilmore and Rosemarie Huber is a book that studies the relationship between a child's developmental age when entering school and his academic success. The authors write: "Much of the research we will review compares elementary school children who at the time they entered school were less than five years three months of age when enrolled in kindergarten or six years three months when enrolled in first grade (often called *summer children* because their birthdays fall between June and September) with children who were as much as six years three months old at kindergarten entrance or seven years three months when they started first grade. To summarize this research very briefly:

1. The chronologically older children in a grade tend to receive many more above-average grades from teachers.
2. Older children also are much more likely to score in the above-average range on standardized achievement tests.
3. The younger children in a grade are far more likely to have failed at least one grade than are older children.
4. The younger children in a grade are far more likely to have been referred by teachers for learning disabilities testing and subsequently have been diagnosed as being learning disabled than are older students in a grade.
5. The academic problems of younger children who were developmentally not ready at school entrance often last throughout their school careers and sometimes even into adulthood."

Not Ready For Kindergarten

If the parents and the nursery school teacher agree that a child is developmentally young for a traditional kindergarten program, what are the options? One choice is for the child to spend another year in nursery school. For some children, and families, this will be comfortable as well as possible. For others, it is uncomfortable and not viable mainly because of the cost of nursery school.

Another option that is increasingly being offered by school systems comes under several names such as pre-kindergarten, transition kindergarten or *young fives* class. This is a *bridge* program for five-year-olds who are simply developmentally young. It runs the full school year for either half-day or full-day classes. For these *young fives* emphasis is on oral and motor skills and both fine and gross motor skills. The focus is to allow these children to test their capacities and skills within the school environment; to build self-confidence for taking on the challenges of academic learning. With more rest and play periods than in kindergarten, *young fives* are given the chance to feel comfortable in the school environment and become competent learners.

Children in pre-kindergarten are promoted the next year into either a kindergarten program or pre-first program.

In some systems the kindergarten is designed as a two-year program. In this two-tier program all five-year-olds enter kindergarten at the same time. Throughout the year, each child is assessed and observed to determine their developmental level. Children who are ready move on to first grade after one year. Children who need extra time remain in kindergarten. If the first year was a half-day program, the second might be a full day. Still another option is keeping your child at home for an extra year. This is a viable option if one parent is at home and there are playmates in the neighborhood or community. Unfortunately, staying at home is not realistic for most families today.

Not Ready For First Grade

One of the most widely offered options in school systems around the country is an *extra year* between kindergarten and first grade. Called pre-first, transition first, junior first or a readiness year, these programs address the needs of six-year-olds who are developmentally young and not ready for the demands of a traditional first grade.

Like kindergarten, these programs are activity-oriented and rich in hands-on materials. Math, writing and reading skills are introduced to these children, who are eager to learn. Later in the year many of these children will be ready to move, without stress, into more formalized reading, math and writing.

In the book, *One Piece of the Puzzle, A Practical Guide for Schools Interested in Implementing a School Readiness Program*, Barbara Carll and Nancy Richard describe a pre-first program in detail. They lists fifteen objectives of the pre-first grade room:

To give the child time to grow.

To help the child develop a strong sense of self—to allow her to *blossom from within.*

To provide an environment rich in equipment and materials where experiences are direct and concrete, to build the foundation for later, more abstract experiences.

To provide movement experiences for development of physical and motor skills.

To promote growth in visual, auditory, and tactile perception—to sharpen the senses.

To provide an opportunity to learn and practice patterning of all kinds—visual, auditory, kinesthetic.

To provide listening activities.

To provide many and varied opportunities for oral expression.

To build a foundation for sophisticated math concepts through manipulation of concrete materials.

To build a foundation for chemistry, physics and biology through discovery and play with blocks and natural materials such as water and sand.

To help the child relate to others socially and to be a part of a group.

To help the child develop problem-solving techniques.

To promote creative expression through art, dance, music, cooking, storytelling.

To help the child develop the habit of success.

To help the child establish an environment of beauty, order and stability.

Transition Two: A Step Between First And Second Grade

The idea of offering an alternative program that allows extra time between first and second grade is just beginning to surface. In addition to pre-kindergarten and pre-first, a growing number of school systems are implementing pre-second programs for developmentally young seven-year-olds.

Who might benefit from a pre-two experience? A very verbal but developmentally young seven-year-old girl who *talked her way into kindergarten* and through first grade is typical of who would benefit. During the spring of first grade, this child appears to peak. She progresses academically, but the social, emotional and physical strain of keeping her position in class is preventing her from reaching her full potential.

There are many bright children whose immaturity does not become apparent in school for several years. Developmental youngness is overlooked because the child has a facade of academic prowess. Immaturity often becomes evident when the child reaches third grade and the curriculum demands change and increase. For these bright young children, who may be at risk when they reach third grade, it would be wise to consider the option of transition second rather than letting the child struggle in grade three.

COMBINATION GRADE: MULTI-AGE GROUPING

Some school systems offer combination grades—two grades in one room. In this setting, all children are in the same room with the same teacher for a two-year period. That way, developmentally young children in a first/second grade combination would spend two years with one teacher. If at the end of this period, a child was not yet ready for third grade, she could be placed in another first/second grade combination with a different teacher, thus giving her the extra year she needs.

Ideally, the new teacher would pick up where the other left off so there would be little repeating of material.

THE IMPORTANCE OF UNDERSTANDING OPTIONS

These programs are not considered retention. But, because most parents didn't have transition programs when they went to school, it might be hard for them to accept a transition class as a positive move. In addition, many parents are not aware of how intense the curriculum has become in the primary grades in the last twenty years. It is very important, then, that schools help parents to understand why these programs exist and how they benefit their children. To cultivate understanding, many school systems conduct regular sessions on child development and transition programs.

In my school, we found that having a booklet on hand with answers to some of the questions parents asked about our pre-first grade program was extremely helpful. We also sent this booklet home to all kindergarten parents in early spring. Here are some of the questions from the booklet.

Q. My child has been examined and I am told he is developmentally young and it is suggested that he go to the pre-first grade. What did I do wrong?
A. The fact that your child is not ready for first

grade is not a reflection on you or your child. You did nothing wrong! What is wrong is the unrealistic expectation that all children are ready for the same school program simply because they are the same chronological age. Each child has his own rate and pattern of growth.

The "information age" and the pressures of our times have stepped up the curriculum, which is making almost impossible demands on children.

Q. How come we are just hearing about all this now? They didn't worry about it when I was going to school?

A. The main reason is because we know a lot more about child development than we did a few years ago.

Another reason is that we are in the "information age" and the pressures of the times have caused a stepping up of curriculum, which is making greater, almost impossible demands on children. We have forgotten the human child as we make technological advances. Because life today is extremely stressful, we want to insure a successful school experience for all children so they continue to enjoy learning throughout their lives.

Q. Is it true that boys and girls develop at different rates?

A. Yes. At the age of six, boys are, on an average, half a year less mature than girls of the same chronological age. At the age of twelve they are one year less mature.

Q. There are three summer months left before

school starts. What can I do to mature my child so he will be ready?
A. You can't make your child ready because you can't mature him. TIME is the chief ingredient of maturity. This is something you cannot hasten.

Frustration and excessive pressure tend to shut off learning and inhibit development.

Q. If my child is immature already, how is he going to mature in a pre-first grade program?
A. In a good environment your child will feel contented and free to develop as fast as nature intended him to. A person learns more when he is enjoying it. Frustration and excessive pressure tend to shut off learning and inhibit development.

What might seem to be play in the pre-first grade is actually very carefully planned and organized exercise. To the child, it is work. The Readiness Room cannot, nor is it meant to, mature your child. It will provide good solid learning experiences that address her level of maturity and inspire future learning.

Q. If my child is borderline, that is, almost ready, but not quite, should he go into pre-first grade?
A. When in doubt, give him the extra year. It can only be beneficial. Give him this extra time to mature.

Q. I feel my child is ready for first grade. The exam says she is five years old developmentally, but she is already reading (in fact, she taught herself). Why shouldn't she go to first grade?
A. This is a very good question because you have

brought up the difference between learning readiness and school readiness. Learning is a continual process from birth on, and at some point on this continuum children are ready to learn academics. For many children, readiness for learning academics occurs long before they are ready to go to school.

There is a difference between learning readiness and school readiness.

School readiness, however, requires more than the ability to do academics. You see, coping with first grade expectations requires the mature forces of the child's social, physical, emotional and neurological being as well as his mature intellect. Your child needs more time to develop in these areas.

Q. What about challenge? Doesn't that count anymore?
A. Challenge is very important, but only when it is felt within the child himself. Challenge imposed from the outside by someone else, will usually have a negative effect. Insurmountable challenge only discourages the child and turns him away from learning. Challenges hard enough to excite the child and easy enough to be conquered will encourage him to rise to the next challenge.

Q. What shall I tell my child, who has been expecting to start first grade and now is going instead to pre-first grade?
A. Most young children accept this placement if their parents do. It is what you feel that is important—your attitude will speak louder than anything you say. Be honest with your child in

discussing your decision for placement. Tell him that this class is where he will be the happiest and that it is the best place for him.

Q. It seems to me that this is babying children. Don't you believe that children could be made to learn?

A. Children in the pre-first grade are learning all the time! They are developing skills that form the foundation for structured academics later on.

As an example, oral language (listening and speaking) is the foundation upon which written language (reading and writing) is built. A child in the pre-first grade will spend more time developing skills of oral language so when he is asked to learn written language, he will learn much faster and more thoroughly.

Contrary to common thought, overall readiness for school is not measured by knowing how to count, how to write, how to hold a pencil, or when to raise one's hand.

Q. As parents, what can we teach our child so she will be ready? What does she need to know to be ready?

A. She needs to know she is an accepted, worthwhile person in the eyes of those she loves. She needs to know that when she goes to this new place, school, she will be treated with dignity and understanding; that she will be met on her own terms and move on from there.

Contrary to common thought, overall readiness for school is not measured by knowing how to count, how to write, how to hold a pencil, or when to raise one's hand. Rather, it is having the maturity to cope with the world and learn at the same time. It is doubtful that teaching him *things* will bring about his maturation. Instead, this kind of pushing is very apt to cause inhibitions that could make him shut off his own development.

You can best get him ready by giving him what he needs NOW, not what he will need next year.

Special Needs Of Disadvantaged Children

There are many children who from infancy have suffered malnutrition or the inherited effect of drugs and neglect. Their opportunity for physical, social, emotional and intellectual development has been limited and when they reach school age, they are far behind other children their age. Many nutritionally deprived children also have health problems that cause frequent absenteeism.

Early intervention in the preschool years is a must for these children. But even with early intervention, it is unreasonable to expect all children to suddenly catch up. If they are to be successful in school, they too, if developmentally young, need time to complete the curriculum. It is not uncommon for these children to take three years to complete kindergarten and first grade rather than the traditional two years.

SPECIAL NEEDS OF NON-ENGLISH-SPEAKING CHILDREN

Children who don't speak English before they come to school may need extra time as well as special programs to help them handle school work in what, for them, is a *foreign* language. Bilingual children also have a right to materials that respect their culture.

Sending children to the next grade before they are ready, setting them up for failure, does not resolve the problems of discrimination. If anything, it makes these problems worse.

EXTRA YEAR PROGRAMS: DISCRIMINATION OR A CHILD'S RIGHT

Is developmental placement, transition classes or grade re-placement discriminatory? Some educators claim it is. While it is true that the percentage of re-placement among poor children and minorities is higher than the general population, that is hardly an argument to deny children correct grade placement. One teacher reported that her School Board cried discrimination and used it as a shield to avoid paying for the extra year of kindergarten or first grade that so many of these children desperately needed.

Sending children to first grade before they are ready, setting them up for failure, does not resolve the problems of discrimination. If anything, it makes these problems worse.

CHAPTER 7
Alternative Options Throughout The Grades

Since each child is a special and unique individual, there is no one right answer for all children or even for children with a similar profile or problem.

How, then, do you come to a decision when you are faced with a child who is having school problems? First of all—and though it is obvious, it bears saying again—watch and listen to the child. Much of what a child feels about himself is expressed through behavior. Also, pay attention to what you feel intuitively, because it's valuable information.

Testing helps. Tests identify particular problems that interfere with learning, such as hearing or vision problems, allergies or neurologically based learning disabilities. Many of these tests, however, are designed to measure only one or two facets of a child's personality or ability and cannot always factor in vital elements of a child's environment or family situation.

Again, paying attention to what you feel intuitively and educating yourself through your child's school, books and other materials will make you aware of all the options available to you. Although re-placement has worked for many children, it isn't necessarily the best option for all. Let's look at some alternatives for those children who would not benefit from re-placement.

REMEDIATION

A remedial program can either be a pullout program where the child goes to a special room or person for extra help, or where the specialist goes into the classroom to work with small groups or individuals. These programs are designed for children who need additional help with skills for a variety of reasons. With the increase of remediation programs, schools are beginning to understand that children have many different learning styles that require alternative instruction and materials.

Remedial programs are based on the premise that the child has not been able to learn particular skills as they were originally presented in the classroom. Educators basically repeat these skills, but pay closer attention to the problems the child encounters so they can present the materials in a way that suits the child. It is one way of helping children with identifiable learning styles and disabilities, since more attention is given to exactly how these children can best learn. This is a positive experience when the extra help does in fact provide the child with success.

One dilemma a teacher may face with remediation is that, while the child needs the extra help, he might resent leaving the room or being separated from the group. You need to find ways to help the child save face because such resentment can stand in the way of learning.

Using remedial services to keep an overplaced child in the wrong grade is a misuse of the service.

Remediation clearly signals to a child that a problem exists. If the *problem* is that the child is developmentally young and not ready for the material, then remediation is not a wise alternative to re-placement. Using remedial services to keep an overplaced child in the wrong grade is a misuse of these services, especially when there is limited space available in these programs. It is unfair to the unready child as well as the other children who truly need the remedial help.

Summer School

Summer school has a certain mystique about it. Some of you might think of summer school as a repair shop or a place that tunes up a child's unsatisfactory academic pattern.

When summer school is used as an alternative to re-placement and a child is taking academic subjects that she didn't complete in the school year, the gain is immediate and short-term. It could be a good solution for children who missed a good deal of school due to illness or an accident. It could be the solution for a child who, though in school, was not really with it because the year had been emotionally upsetting for him. Summer school works best for these children who need to learn the academic skills they missed during the year.

A developmentally young child will not magically catch up in four to six weeks.

There are several things summer school will not accomplish, however. If the child is developmentally young in the social, emotional and physical areas of development, summer school can do nothing to speed this up. Children will grow over the summer, but at a rate no faster than thirty days a month. A developmentally young child will not magically catch up in four to six weeks.

There are summer school programs that are primarily recreational and enrichment oriented and are not intended as an alternative to re-placement. These programs are usually enjoyable and rewarding. If any of these programs, such as sports, music or creative arts, builds on an area where your child does well and experiences success, encourage him to take part. The better your child feels about himself, the more energy he has for coping when school begins.

EXTRA HOMEWORK

For a child who is overplaced, additional homework as an alternative to correct grade placement is a poor remedy. It might help the child struggle through, but it will not put the child in sync with the curriculum nor will it ease the stress that overplacement creates. In fact, extra homework will increase stress.

The option of special homework to solve a school problem can work if the parents are ready to be actively involved in it. They would be taking on the role of tutors.

For a child who is overplaced, additional homework as an alternative to correct grade placement is a poor remedy.

If parents have the time and interest to do this kind of tutoring and if they enjoy it, a lot can be achieved. Children benefit not only by understanding the material better but also from the interest and concern demonstrated by their parents.

If there are pressures on the parent's time, for whatever reason, there is a risk that the extra time it takes to do this homework will generate stress and frustration. If the homework becomes an obvious and irritating burden, the results are counterproductive. The child is now struggling to learn and also feels she is losing love.

PRIVATE TUTORING

Tutoring after school or on Saturday seems to be a popular option that parents choose when they realize that their child is having trouble learning and keeping up with school work. It has been encouraged by the vast number of commercial tutoring services that have sprung up in recent years. With advertisements promising success, they imply that they know a secret for efficient learning that the public schools don't know.

If there are specific academic skills with which a child needs extra help, tutoring can be helpful. It can help with short-term remedial goals. If tutoring is in connection with a recognized clinic that works with learning disabilities or underachievement, there is value in learning more about the causes of the child's school problem. Special Education mandated by law is available through the public schools for long-term help.

Tutoring is a poor substitute for correct grade placement.

Tutoring is a poor substitute for correct grade placement. The child might *make it* in the wrong grade for long periods of time because tutoring shores up academic scores. But, a child will probably not develop into an independent, self-confident learner this way. Tutoring cuts into a child's *free time,* which can cause resentment, particularly if there is no end in sight.

Individual Education Plan

An Individual Education Plan, IEP, is generally thought of in connection with special education, since it is mandated for all handicapped children by the Education for All Handicapped Children Act of 1975. The IEP has also been found to be effective with non-handicapped children.

IEPs are usually written by a team that includes the child's teacher, the school psychologist and other specialists. The parents may be involved, and if not, they would certainly review the plan with the teacher. Individual tests are also part of setting up the program and assessing growth.

The plan outlines academic and behavioral goals and objectives and the methods and strategies to attain them. It is always open to revision and is reviewed periodically by the team. This kind of in-depth evaluation and planning for a child should help to resolve some problems.

Unfortunately, while IEPs are required for identifiable handicapped children, there are many dysfunctional children who do not fall into this category. Individualized programs for non-handicapped children might be possible where classes are small. In schools with large class size and limited staff, developing and carrying out IEPs for non-handicapped children is often not feasible.

Promotion On Trial

Promotion to the next grade, on trial, is often urged by parents who cling to the hope that somehow their child will catch up. A mature child with a solid academic history who has lost ground because of an accident or illness might well be served by being promoted *on condition*, but the *condition* really rests on the teacher and parents who must help the child catch up. If a child is developmentally young, it is not a question of regaining lost ground or catching up. The child is struggling because she is overplaced.

Promotion on *trial* or *on probation* should be used with caution because it carries a heavy message. It clearly says that the child is to blame for failing and on top of this, the child is now 100 percent responsible for turning this situation around next year. If he doesn't, the *punishment* will be to go back a grade. During the year, the child will look over his shoulder, wonder when the axe will fall—when he will be sent back. This burden of responsibility is too great for any young child. No child deserves to be put on trial, especially when he has done nothing wrong.

REPEAT AND LATER PROMOTE

This rests on the assumption that there might be a growth spurt and the child will catch up. Some children do have growth spurts and if the child continues to be uncomfortable or unhappy in the re-placement grade, another move is an option. However, if the original re-placement put the child in a comfortable learning situation, the spurt of academic growth will provide solid success and a sense of accomplishment.

There is a danger in *promotion later on*. It puts a negative cast on the re-placement by raising expectations that the child might not be able to meet, again disappointing herself, her parents and her teacher.

TRACKING

Tracking, the discriminatory grouping of children by *ability,* was once a widespread practice, but relatively few school systems use it today. Tracking would begin in the lower grades with group names such as *Bluebirds, Robins,* and the inevitable bottom track which might as well have been called the *Buzzards.* Unfortunately, once a Buzzard, always a Buzzard. A child was kept in that bottom track right through high school. Some school systems still have some form of tracking, but it is a poor choice to use that lower track as an option to repeating a grade.

PRIVATE SCHOOL

One option for children who are having trouble in public or large school settings is to go to a private school. Private schools, more often than not, offer small classes and most can provide more individualized instruction.

Some parents who do not accept the recommendation of re-placement opt to send their child to private school. One parent confessed that she moved her child to a private school out of anger only to learn that he had carried his immaturity with him and was accepted on the condition that he repeat a grade. It is not unusual for private schools to move a child back a grade upon enrollment. Some children benefit from a new setting when re-placed, particularly if the structure or style of teaching is better suited to their learning style.

It's also not uncommon for educators in private schools to encourage a post-graduate year for high school students who need more time to mature or perhaps strengthen academic skills before going on to college.

Highly Structured Programs

Some students prosper in a rigid traditional classroom setting where the main emphasis is on a direct instructional method. This seems to be effective for children who have difficulty staying on task and attending to their work. However, it is important for these children to be encouraged to develop some independence and self-regulation so they will not fall apart when they graduate from this highly structured setting.

Programs For different Learning Styles

Recent research has identified different but equally valid learning styles. A child who has trouble learning math with pencil and paper, for example, might pick it up easily when taught with manipulatives. A child who learns one way but not another isn't being uncooperative, nor does it mean that he has a learning disability. Discussing this in her book *Smart Kids with School Problems: Things to Know and Ways to Help*, Priscilla L. Vail writes: "Often a smart kid's school problem arises from a mismatch between his learning style and the methods and materials used in the curriculum. When this happens, it is the student who is diagnosed as learning disabled, instead of the materials being labeled inappropriate."

CONTRACT TEACHING

Some teachers have successfully used what is called an *education contract*. Developed with parents and child, an education contract outlines specific goals and objectives for the child to strive for. Academic skills as well as conduct are covered in the contract.

Since it is developed and signed by the parents, child and teacher, it tends to clarify and confirm the child's strengths and weaknesses, what needs to be worked on and how it will be done.

A sensitive child who is already feeling pressure is not a good candidate for contract teaching, because it is intimidating. This child may feel singled out and view the contract as punishment.

HOME SCHOOLING

The home schooling option has gained popularity in recent years. There is a small, yet significant number of children who, for a variety of reasons, benefit from a year or more of home instruction. A good profile of such a child would be a very sensitive student who, if repeated in a school setting, might suffer severe emotional stress that would far outweigh any positive benefits of re-placement.

One book that has been immensely helpful to parents seeking home schooling is *Home Spun Children*. The authors, Raymond S. and Dorothy N. Moore, are pioneers, respectively, in the fields of developmentally appropriate education and grade placement.

POST-GRADUATE PROGRAMS

A post-graduate year of high school is offered by a number of schools. In this fifth year, which is taken after graduation, students who have barely made it through high school have a chance to polish skills, correct deficiencies, and just plain mature. Many are children who perhaps should have repeated a grade many years before but didn't. They have struggled through but would be courting disaster if they immediately enrolled in college. For those students who choose to do a post-grad year, their chances of dropping out of college are decreased.

Delayed College Entrance

Today colleges and universities are willing to consider applications for delayed entrance from students who choose to take a year off between high school graduation and college. This is a year for getting things together educationally, emotionally, physically and socially.

What can a student do for a year? The opportunities are abundant—work, travel, take local community education courses, participate in an Outward Bound Program, be an exchange student in a foreign country, do volunteer work, be an apprentice or do an internship in a field of interest.

Students who have chosen this feel good about themselves during their year off. When asked what they are doing after high school, they can reply "I'm going to college, but I'm not going until next year."

CHAPTER 8 Teachers And The Fine Art Of Re-placement

Retention can be a negative experience, and handled in the traditional way, it is likely to be. How, then, can we make retention into a positive experience?

It is not enough to just call it *re-placement.* It can't be done by changing the words but not the intent. You have to look at retention in a totally different way. You have to change your ideas and expectations about it. These changes, and they are big changes, must start with the teacher, then the parents, and finally the child. Change of any kind is generally stressful and sometimes even painful. But when teachers, parents, and children get to the point where they can understand and handle retention as *re-placement*—something positive—a second chance at success, an opportunity—the results can be phenomenal!

The components that make this process of change successful are time, dialogue, and listening.

Take time to think about the situation, to share information and observations and to consider the options. Teachers, parents and the child all need to be part of the re-placement decision. An ongoing dialogue between teacher and parents, between parents and child and between teacher and child is vital. And everyone needs to listen. The adults need to be attentive both to their own feelings and those of the child.

INTRODUCING THE IDEA OF RE-PLACEMENT

You can bet that re-placement is almost always brought up by the teacher. So seldom do parents raise this suggestion that when they do, it often catches the teacher off-balance momentarily. A typical response is to quickly reassure the parent and dispel the idea of re-placement. Be careful to avoid this response and take time to understand what has prompted the parent's suggestion.

As I said, far more often it is the teacher who suggests the unwelcome news of re-placement. Telling parents that their child is immature, developmentally young, and not ready for the kindergarten or first grade curriculum is, to say the least, hard. And it doesn't get easier. A teacher can expect that parents will be upset. Grade re-placement always raises anxiety levels and produces more stress than almost any other topic. No parent ever gets steamed up over a teacher individualizing math or reading programs. But let the teacher suggest that their child needs more time to do the curriculum, and parents experience emotions they never knew they had!

No matter how gently the parents are told, the reaction is usually the same—total disappointment.

Parents of kindergartners experience anxiety just letting go of their child. Then, no sooner have they let go, than they learn that their child is going to get what they perceive as the *Pink Slip*. Help! They feel that their child is rejected, not working to capacity, not making the grade. No matter how gently the parents are told, the reaction is usually the same—total disappointment.

THE HARDEST PART OF THE JOB

It's tough to be the bearer of this kind of news. It's much easier to duck the issue, say nothing, and send the whole class on to the next grade—ready or not. But that's a cop-out. Who suffers? The struggling, overplaced children do. But so do the teachers.

Teachers experience a lot of anguish when they have overplaced children in their classroom. They are under tremendous pressure to have their children score well on standardized achievement tests and to complete the grade level work. As we know by now, overplaced children are not yet ready for what is being taught which only adds to the teacher's tension. Teachers agonize in March when they have to make a decision whether to recommend re-placement or just move the child along. It's distressing to know that you are passing children and feeling that you are setting them up for failure.

In ancient Greece they beheaded the bearer of bad news. Parents aren't allowed to go that far, thank goodness.

In ancient Greece they beheaded the bearer of bad news. Although parents aren't allowed to go that far, thank goodness, teachers still dread informing parents—and with good reason. The news that their child might repeat a grade elicits a wave of emotions. Their greatest fear has materialized: their child has failed; the family is disgraced. When emotions run high, negative reactions are to be expected. It's not uncommon for a parent to attack the teacher verbally. And if they don't, that still doesn't mean that they will accept the news easily.

Alert Parents As Soon As Possible

Since the teacher can expect the first conference to be uncomfortable and stressful, it is easy to put it off, but don't. Sometimes when the teacher forewarns the parents early in the year, they will say that the teacher hasn't given the child enough time to really shine. They often feel the teacher has given up on the child, doesn't understand him or doesn't like him for some reason. On the other hand, the single, most common parent complaint is: "Why wasn't I told sooner that there was a problem?" It's a teacher's *Catch 22*.

"Simply put, the entire question of retention should not be dropped in parents' laps at the last minute." writes Anthony D. Fredericks in his article "Retention: Keeping Parents Informed". "As one who has retained kids, made recommendations regarding retention and been retained himself, I'm very sensitive to the *failure factor*. Being suddenly informed that all the effort, time and energy put into the school year have gone for naught can be highly traumatic. Egos are bruised, feelings are hurt and, in the minds of some, a whole year has been lost. To counteract such feelings, we need to take a positive approach, keep up an active dialogue and start the dialogue as early as possible."

Alerting parents early in the year fulfills a moral obligation and gives parents more time to come to an understanding of what's involved, before they must make a decision.

Mrs. Humphries is a veteran kindergarten teacher. Two or three weeks into the new school year, she is aware of several children who are young for kindergarten. "Myra is still having a particularly hard time parting from her mother each morning and Charlie is constantly taking in-house field trips. He is a happy-go-lucky little kid who can't be held still very long. Kindergarten is too structured for his developmental age. Ken is a typical *late bloomer*, smart enough but just not ready to take on the kindergarten curriculum."

Mrs. Humphries scheduled a conference with Myra's mother right away and with Charlie and Ken's parents in late November or December.

Experienced teachers frequently spot over-placed children early in the year. For some of these children, immediate re-placement would be the best course of action. And as with all re-placement, it's easier in the younger grades.

I've known cases where young children seem to sense where they belong. Bruce was one of these children. One day early in the year after recess, his first grade teacher discovered Bruce was missing. He hadn't come in from recess. She searched the room, searched the bathrooms. She sent an aide out to search the playground in case he hadn't heard the bell. They checked the nurse's office, but no Bruce. By this time the teacher was getting a little panicky. She notified the principal who came right down. As they talked with the class, one of the children suggested Bruce might be with his friends, whom he played with at recess; they were in the pre-first grade class. So, the principal checked the pre-first grade class. There was Bruce, sitting in one of the activity centers working busily. There is so much activity and movement in a transition program that the pre-first teacher hadn't realized that she had taken on another passenger after recess. When they asked Bruce what he was doing there, he said this is what he liked to do.

He liked being with his friends and he wanted to stay and not go back to his classroom. At the end of kindergarten, pre-first had been recommended for Bruce, but his parents did not accept that recommendation at that time. After this event, however, they reconsidered and Bruce was re-placed.

A teacher, experienced or inexperienced, in whatever grade, knows by February or March if a child is not really able to keep up with the work. At this time, retention or some other option should be considered for discussion for the coming year.

PARENT CONFERENCING

Now that a conference is in order, when will it be? Traditionally parent conferences are scheduled after school hours, but this can add to the strain on the teacher, who may be completely exhausted after a full day of teaching. Fortunately, parents are often willing to meet at other times. Consider meeting with them before school or during a free period when everyone has a higher energy level. Stand ready to make a house call if necessary. This may be the only feasible way to meet both parents together. A house call is an indication to the parents of a deep level of caring on the part of the teacher.

In scheduling the conference, it is important for the teacher to give an overview of what the concern is and what the teacher feels they should discuss. Yes, the parents might get their defenses up. But if the parents don't know what is to be discussed, the mystery can be unsettling and all too often they will conjure up the worst scenario. The real business of the conference is then clouded by that scenario.

When Mrs. Humphries called Ken's mother she said, "Mrs. Robinson, I'd like to arrange a time when I could talk with you and Mr. Robinson. Ken is a fine boy with a good sense of humor and he is also young for kindergarten and experiencing much stress. I want to talk with you about the potential problems he could face if he is assigned to first grade next year."

When the second grade teacher called Bert's mother she said: "Mrs. Sharp, I'd like to arrange a time when I could talk with you about Bert. He has been really trying these first few weeks of school. It's a struggle, however, for him to keep up. Bert has some problems with school work that stem, I suspect, from being in the wrong grade. I think Bert is overplaced and I want to discuss how that is affecting him and also what we might do to correct the situation. I have several solutions for you to consider."

Set A Tone That Indicates Respect And Concern

Listed below are several things to keep in mind that will relieve some of the stress of the conference. The first four assume that the conference will be at the school. The fifth, which spells out useful ground rules, would apply for a home visit as well.

1. Pick a reasonably comfortable setting. Make every effort to hold the conference where phone calls and ringing bells are at a minimum. Having a delicate conversation interrupted is maddening and, to some parents, insulting.

2. Offer refreshments such as coffee, tea, or soda. I frequently had conferences in the morning before school and would pick up donuts on the way. Refreshments help to put parents at ease.

3. Don't sit behind a desk or opposite the parents across a table. Furniture between two parties sends a non-verbal signal that a confrontation is expected. This discussion doesn't have a right and a wrong side—you are both considering what is best for the child.

4. Handle the first conference by yourself. Too many school officials can be intimidating to most parents. If the child has some unusual school problems and the guidance counselor or another specialist has important insights to offer, you might want to have them join in for part of the conference. In that case,

try to give the parents time to review what they've heard. Encourage them to think about options and take time in making their decision.

5. Articulate the following ground rules, as obvious as they might seem, both at the beginning of the conference and, if needed, as the conference progresses. It will make the parents more comfortable.
   - The point of the meeting is to help their child.
   - Their opinion and knowledge of their child is important to the teacher.
   - No matter what happens at the meeting, they make the final decision. Encourage them to take as much time as they need to make that decision. Don't set a deadline if you can avoid it.
   - You will respect and support whatever decision they make.
   - Both of you could change your opinion at a later date as new information comes to light. (This is another reason why parent conferences on the issue of re-placement should not be left until late in the school year.)

- Agree to the fact that you may disagree, and, if there is a major difference of opinion, you will attempt to negotiate the differences. (If you sense beforehand that the parents are particularly resistant to accepting the fact that their child might have problems, handle this at the beginning.)
- Agree to discuss what is presented. If the conference goes sour, adjourn it and recommence at a future date.

Present Your Concerns

Demonstrate the cause for your concern with notes that outline specific observations of behavior. If possible, have test results on hand. In kindergarten, this could be a developmental readiness test. In older grades, this would be classroom tests as well as standardized tests or special tests given by the guidance counselor. Have examples of class work together with information from other teachers who might work with the child.

Note specifics such as the child's ability to focus or stay on task. This way you can give the parents something concrete to consider. Always be truthful, even though it might provoke strong emotions.

Check your vocabulary! When you are talking about a child who is developmentally young and overplaced, don't inadvertently use words that indicate a neurological problem.

For instance, avoid saying:

"Your child is a slow learner."

"Your child is hyperactive."

"Your child has a developmental delay or lag."

Take a firm grip on your self-confidence and remember that you are a caring professional.

Avoid phrases like *lazy, isn't trying hard enough,* and *isn't shaping up.* Help parents avoid using them. These imply that the child is at fault and that's not the case. The behavior and learning difficulties of an overplaced child stem from a cause that the child has no control over. The child can't change the cause, but the teacher and parents can. The purpose of your conference is to explore ways to remedy the situation.

Try to avoid educational jargon. State the issues in clear, concise, straightforward terms. When you use terms like *developmental age* or *developmentally young,* have clear definitions in everyday language to help parents grasp these important concepts.

Take a firm grip on your self-confidence and remember that you are a caring professional. You have given concrete signs of overplacement and you have shared your subjective observations and intuitive sense of the child. Don't apologize for this. Teacher observation, though subjective, is highly predictive of ongoing school success or difficulty. If the conference is about re-placing a child in first, second, or one of the higher grades, be sure to make all the options available for parents to consider. Be open to trying what the parents suggest. There is never one right way to do anything. Chapters 6 and 7 discuss some of the options that are available.

Don't take parents' comments too personally.

Don't take parents' comments too personally. Under strain, they, like the ancient Greeks, may wish to cut off your head. But, since that's not allowed, don't be surprised if they lash out at you with uncalled-for remarks, insinuations or accusations. Chalk those words up to their disappointment. Don't harbor them, waiting, perhaps, for an apology. Remember, you have accomplished something for the child in taking this first step. Now, if progress is to be made, you must stay open and supportive of the parents.

Throughout this conference, you have tried to tell parents that their child is a fine child who has school problems. The teacher's judgment, as in the case of Mrs. Humphries, is that the child is overplaced. In another case it might be that the child has a learning disability, or you may have detected a problem with the child's hearing or vision. Do not be surprised if the parent seems to hear only part of what is said. Everyone resists bad news.

After the parents leave, they are quite likely to ask themselves, "What exactly did the teacher say?" Have something that the parents can take with them that explains their particular issue. Give them another chance to digest by reading about what you, the teacher, feel is involved.

Don't pull rank on parents who are adamantly opposed to re-placement.

Don't pull rank on parents who are adamantly opposed to re-placement. You will run into parents, on occasion, who are not upset and disappointed by the idea of re-placement; they are adamantly opposed. Present your case. If they will have none of it, don't try to *win*. A serious confrontation with adamant parents is apt to cause so much trouble that it could jeopardize your pre-kindergarten/pre-first transition program or your re-placement policy. Do, however, document what happens. Write down something to the effect that on a particular date I recommended to these parents that their child be given an extra year in the particular grade. I made this offer and they declined. Present this document to the parents and ask them to sign it. Should they refuse, you sign it and ask someone to witness your signature. There should be no question at some future time as to whether or not the parents had been informed.

Most parents will listen, try to understand the situation, and want to work with the school in finding the best solution for their child.

A Word To Parents: How To Get The Most Out Of The Conference

When Ellie Robinson hung up the phone she just stood there, numb. The call was from the kindergarten teacher, Mrs. Humphries, asking for a conference to discuss her son Ken. Apparently he wasn't doing well in kindergarten. She stood there hurt, disappointed, afraid because she wanted things to go smoothly for Ken. He was a lovable child, a wonderful little person, and he deserved to have things go well for him. She had secretly feared that Ken might be having a hard time in school.

When Harry Robinson got home that night and heard about the up-coming conference, he dispelled some of her worry. How could Ken be too young for kindergarten? Ridiculous! He was five in August. He had had three years in nursery school. He's a bright kid. Alright, he's a little slower than the other kids at learning some things, but, given time, he catches on. She just needs to give him another month or so and he'll be at the top of the class.

When the Robinsons heard that Mrs. Humphries was asking them to consider having Ken wait a year before entering first grade, it was a blow. No, she didn't think things would change in a month or two; there were too many signs that he was young and overplaced. Yes, they would have time to talk about it as the year progressed, but meanwhile they should keep in mind what this all meant for Ken.

When you are called by the teacher to come in for a conference and the reason isn't clear, ask. Even if you dread bad news, not knowing allows your imagination to conjure up something probably far worse.

It is hard not to go into such a conference on the defensive, but try to keep an open mind. Give the teacher the benefit of the doubt. Don't take your friends' and neighbors' word for what she's going to say or what you ought to say. Listen to what the teacher has to say. Hold off putting up your defenses or making a final decision until all the facts are in. The teacher has initiated the conference for exactly the same reason you have come to it. You both want to do what is best for your child.

You both want what is best for the child.

The Teacher Needs To Know Your Questions And Concerns

Before going into the conference, make a note of the questions you want to ask. During the conference, the discussion often takes a direction that will miss some of your concerns. Your notes will remind you. It is important for all involved that you truly understand exactly what the teacher is trying to say. Don't hesitate to repeat a question or add, "what do you mean?"

After you have heard the teacher out, and if you feel upset or overwhelmed by the problem, explain this. The teacher needs to understand how you feel and how deeply you hurt.

Share anything that may be upsetting your child at home: it might affect your child's school performance. Even the slightest change in family circumstances can affect your child's ability to function. Also be sure the teacher is aware of any physical or emotional problem that your child is struggling with, such as hearing, vision, allergies or depression because of some family crisis.

As you discuss the possibility of re-placement or other options, let the teacher know if there are points of disagreement between you and your spouse. This holds true at any stage. It is important for your child that both parents support and encourage him if re-placement is to work.

Trust your instincts.

Do you and the teacher have two quite different perceptions of your child? It can appear that way. As parents, you see your child function on a one-to-one basis. The teacher sees your child in the context of a class interacting both with other children and with an organized curriculum. Give the teacher's observations serious thought. Her judgment of your child might appear to be highly subjective, but it grows out of observing many children. There is a high correlation between a teacher's prediction and the child's success in the following grade.

Trust your instincts. You may experience pain and disappointment that will temporarily cloud your vision, but you have a feel for your child's pattern of growth and way of responding. Trust the fact that your intuition will let you know when you are on the right track.

Additional Information

Don't hesitate to ask for more information. You are not the only parents who have never heard of *developmental placement, under-achievers,* or *over-placement.* In an effort to find ways of helping children, educators have created terms to help identify what stands in the way of children's success in school. These terms are of no help to you, however, unless you find out what they mean in everyday language. Do not assume that these are all just kind or fancy words for saying a child is dumb or stupid. Remember that Einstein had difficulty in school too! So, ask for definitions and more information. Become informed. Listed in the back of this book are pamphlets, books, audio and videotapes that explain overplacement and its effects.

Although the teacher is busy, her business is your child. When you have thought about the problem she has outlined, and when other questions come up, ask for another conference.

No matter what you think of the teacher, be careful not to go to the conference with a chip on your shoulder. The teacher might need help, but not a scolding. Don't turn the conference into a debate or fight. You may win, but your child will lose. Whether you agree with the teacher or not, the decision about retention is yours. If you oppose retention, if you opt for another means of addressing the problem, that is largely your decision. In the meantime, if you engage your children in what you feel is *a fight with the school,* you may further erode the child's relationship with the teacher and further sour the child's present school situation. This will decrease his willingness and ability to learn. If you pass your *fight* with the school on to your child, you further handicap the child's ability to gain from his school experience.

CHAPTER 9

Parents' Point Of View On Re-placement

For most parents a child is an extension of themselves. The child's success is their success. The child's happiness adds to their happiness. Conversely, the child's apparent failure is also theirs and it is a terrible disappointment. When, like the Robinsons, parents are told that their child is not ready for first grade, their expectations are knocked down. It's a loss and it evokes a lot of emotion.

THE DECISION IS DIFFICULT

Newspaper editor and publisher, Carl Tucker III, wrote of his and his wife's experience when it was recommended that his son Peter be given another year in kindergarten. It is a good description of the kind of process parents need to go through in making a decision about re-placement.

"When my wife and I were in school, only *stupid* kids got *held back* as we called it. Stupid or maybe spastic. In any event, it was a disgrace—an episode which was whispered about for years after, like a strange disease or a parent's divorce.

When my wife and I were in school, only "stupid" kids got "held back" as we called it.

"In those days, we had never heard about appropriate class placement or, God forbid, learning disabilities. Kids who had trouble keeping up with the class were deficient either in mental power or will power. No matter how unhappy you were in your class, you clung grimly to your place, unwilling to accept the shame of falling back.

"Times have changed. Educators and researchers have come to understand that circumstances may drastically affect a child's ability to learn, and that what appears to be a deficiency may only be a disability, easily overcome.

"As reasonably aware parents, patronizing an enlightened country day school, we were aware of the new sophistication in education. We were familiar with some of the new terms in the educational lexicon like *small motor skills* and *dyslexia* and glad that children with learning problems were getting a fairer shake. We were not, however, prepared for the suggestion that our oldest child, Peter, should be *given another year* in kindergarten.

"The recommendation, indeed, angered us. Both of us, as it happened, had been the youngest in our grade school classes, and had done fine. Why, we wondered, shouldn't Peter do the same?

"We worried about the effects of such a move

on Peter's ego. Wouldn't he be disheartened by this vote of non-confidence, as we interpreted it? Wouldn't he feel like an outcast from his friends? And wouldn't the sense of inferiority triggered by this setback handicap him for the rest of his life?

"Initially, everything the school administrators said on the subject struck us as nonsense. They said Peter was obviously bright, basing their comments on the size of his vocabulary, his long concentration span, his number sense and his supply of general information. They conceded that he was not the lowest scorer in this class on standardized tests, that there were others who scored less well whom they were planning to graduate to first grade. Why then, we wondered, shouldn't Peter be given the chance to tough it out? Didn't competition strengthen character? Would he be better serviced being in a class where everything came easily? Wouldn't repeating a year make him, not a better student, but lazier, over-confident, relaxed?

Initially, everything the school administrators said on the subject struck us as nonsense.

"Granted, we had seen in Peter during this year some signs of strain. An instinctive competitor, he wasn't enjoying his daily challenges at school, and both at school and home, would often engage in infuriating stillness. On the athletic field, he was mindful of his comparatively lackluster performance and disturbed by it. Perhaps most worrisome for parents who work in the newspaper business, Peter seemed to be making no progress toward reading. He refused to even try, and for a time we feared that his precocious younger sister, two years his junior, would learn to read before her older brother.

"We met on several occasions with his school's administrators and learning specialists, who answered our concerns with sympathy and tact. In a sense, they made our decision more difficult by leaving it up to us. Peter, they said, could advance to first grade to keep up with his class. However, because he was both chronologically and developmentally several months younger than the next oldest boy, they predicted that his strain would intensify and his joy in learning would wane, and eventually, possibly as late as fourth grade, the school would be forced to hold him back, which would do much greater harm to his self-esteem. They also assured us that they had never seen such a step turn out to be a mistake, and that parents who had accepted this recommendation were almost unanimously enthusiastic about the results.

"We deliberated long. We concluded that we must either accept the school's recommendations or remove Peter to another school, for who were we to put our hunches in opposition to the advice of experts? We even told the school of our tentative plans to enroll Peter elsewhere.

"In the end, however, we gave in. Peter repeated; and for a few months, his mood was uneasy and no positive results were apparent. Gradually, however, we could see him begin to realize and assume a natural position of leadership in his new group. He took more pleasure in athletics and, happily, maintained his friendships with his best friends in his former grade. By the time he reached first grade (which he playfully suggested that he was not quite ready for), he was ready to read and absorb with an infectious joy. One of his favorite pastimes became writing stories and teaching his younger sister her letters."

PARENTS' PAIN

Some years ago, Elisabeth Kubler-Ross identified five stages that we go through when confronted with loss. We begin with disbelief or denial, progress through anger, turn to bargaining, sink into depression, and finally come to accepting the loss and moving on with what needs to be done in our lives.

We begin with disbelief or denial, progress through anger, turn to bargaining, sink into depression, and finally come to accepting the loss and moving on with what needs to be done in our lives.

Elisabeth Kubler-Ross was writing of the loss and grief connected with death and dying. Some years ago a young mother, who had a child who was repeating kindergarten, pointed out to me that parents go through these same five stages when confronted with the need to have their child repeat a grade. Their disappointment is a loss and parents must give themselves time—and *permission*—to work through the five stages.

The five stages are not linear or hierarchical and there is no specific amount of time set for moving through each stage. Some parents hear the recommendation and quickly arrive at stage five of acceptance. Some parents get bogged down in denial or anger and can't move on. Still others move through the first four stages only to have a friend, neighbor, or relative say something negative which bounces them temporarily back to stage one.

Linda Pass, author of *Taking a Test: The Inside Story,* told me of a reluctant mother who some months after the initial conference, said to the principal, "Don't ever stop telling parents about going through grief. At first it didn't connect, then suddenly I realized why I've been feeling so crazy. I had been going through the first stages of grief all along. Remembering your talk helped me work through my emotions. I've reached Acceptance."

Listed are the five stages along with the thoughts associated with each stage. Reading them won't make you immune to these feelings, but hopefully it will help you to know that it is not just you or your spouse who is suffering and resisting the news.

The point of this process is to rid yourself of the disappointment and hurt, and to clear your vision so that you can see your unique, lovable child as an individual with particular needs that deserve attention.

THE FIVE STAGES: DENIAL, ANGER, BARGAINING, DEPRESSION, ACCEPTANCE

Stage 1. Denial

- This can't happen to us. No one has ever stayed back in our family.
- This notice of possible retention is only a threat to spur our child to do better.
- Our child is too bright to ever be considered for retention.
- The teacher must have a personality conflict with our child.
- Our child just takes a longer time to settle down.
- If our child repeats he'll be 19 when he graduates and that's not feasible.
- We haven't seen any problems at home.
- Our child has been singled out just to make an example for the other children.
- Our child is lazy—the teacher needs to be more demanding.
- We're sure our child is not the only child who is having difficulty.
- Obviously the new teacher doesn't know what he is doing. He just needs a little more experience.
- The observation tool must not be valid or reliable.
- I know they flunk a few children each year to show they have tough standards.

Stage 2. Anger

- The trouble is the schools today don't have high enough standards.
- No child with three years of nursery school should ever have to stay back.
- Why weren't we told of this sooner?
- It is all the fault of the previous teacher—she didn't do her job.
- We pay high enough taxes! The school should teach so that all can pass.
- We should try our child with a more experienced teacher!
- The school has it in for our family.
- The trouble is teachers coddle kids today. Struggle will build character!
- The classroom is overcrowded. Reduce the class size instead of flunking kids.
- No one said school was easy. Let our child work harder.

Stage 3. Bargaining

- Our whole family blooms late. Be patient with our child, she will bloom in high school.
- Why can't the teacher individualize the program for our child?
- If our child shows improvement, we will buy him a bicycle.
- We will have our child tutored at home.
- We will do more homework with our child.
- Our child will attend summer school.

- Maybe we should try private school for a year.
- Maybe our child does need to repeat a year, but this isn't the year to do it.
- Our child only needs a new reading series that is more up to date.
- Our child just needs another chance to catch up.
- What about remedial programs?

Stage 4. Depression

- We have failed our child.
- Our child will carry the stigma of failure forever.
- Our child won't have any friends.
- Our family reputation is tainted.
- How can we ever face our friends, neighbors and relatives?
- Our pride drove us to put her in kindergarten when she was too young.
- We made our child suffer in the wrong grade too long.
- We have been blaming the teacher and the school and we were wrong. How can we ever bring ourselves to apologize?
- How will we ever be able to tell our child?
- If only we had been better parents, our child would have done better in school.
- Our child is not as bright as the other children.

- Our child's size will make him stick out like a sore thumb if he repeats.
- Our child will be too old to play sports in high school.

Stage 5. Acceptance

- We accept our child just the way he is, not how we want him to be.
- If a placement mistake was made, we made it! We will do all in our power to help our child understand she did nothing wrong.
- Every child has the right to correct grade placement. It is our responsibility to assure this right.
- We don't care what the rest of the world thinks...we only want what is best for our child!
- We want our child to enjoy not only school, but life, to the fullest.
- Our child must be given the best opportunity for him.
- We accept our child's self-esteem as paramount to her success.
- We view this extra year as a gift...a second chance.
- We accept that our child has a personal internal time piece that is just right for him. This time piece allows him to develop at his own rate of growth.

- We will not be impatient for our child to grow. We will enjoy every stage.

Some Basic Do's And Don'ts

Don't blame your child. Your child did nothing wrong.

Don't blame yourself. One of the biggest burdens parents have to overcome is guilt. Remember, what is done is done. There is nothing to be ashamed of. Get rid of the guilt and move on. No good will come of feeling guilty.

Don't blame the school. It will not help your child to succeed if you harbor bad feelings about the school.

Both parents should be in agreement. It's important for your child to know from your words and your body language that both Mom and Dad support the decision. Let your child know you think it's a positive idea. Parent support is vital!

Work with the teacher and principal of the school. Let your child realize that "my parents, teachers, and principal—my adult world—cares about me and believes this is best for me." Your child will feel your support and believe the decision is right.

Be the lightning *rod for any static your child receives.* If your child is worried about peer reaction, tell your child to blame you, Mom and Dad. "My Mom and Dad said I had to stay back." This will help your child save face.

Reassure your child that school is going to be easier and more fun from now on. Yes, there might be a little teasing, but that's okay. Your child will be very glad about the extra year.

Learn as much as you can about re-placement. Ask your school for books on the subject. Talk to educators and parents who have re-placed their children. Attend lectures. Once you have background information, trust your intuitive sense. You know what is best for your child.

"Customer Satisfaction" Runs High

When re-placement works and a child is in a comfortable, effective learning situation, it not only eases the stress on the child, but it also lifts a great burden of worry off the parents.

- One parent, Lorraine Braddock, wrote: "After your lecture I got *I Hate School,* read it and shared it with my husband who also heard your lecture.

  "We talked to Nathan on Thursday night and asked him to make up his own mind whether to finish this year in fifth grade or to move back to fourth with his sister. (This was mid-term.) He chose to go back. It made a completely different child of him! Nathan very seldom has homework (work not finished in class) and he sometimes helps his sister with her work.

"His fifth grade teacher also heard your lecture and she handled the transfer just fantastically! She had a small party for Nathan and explained it all to the class just as we did to Nathan. By the end of the party the whole class was saying "Hooray for Nathan!" There have been no hard feelings between any of the students and Nathan."

- It's easy to imagine the relief of getting a good report card after re-placing your child. James's parents had the pleasure of reading these comments from his teachers. "I can't believe this is the same child! I realized that last year whenever I got ready to introduce a new letter or concept, I would build in face-savers and privacy for James because he would get so upset if he made a mistake, or if anyone saw a correction marked on his paper. This year he's what I call Rock and Roll. He's solid as a Rock; I can depend on him. And he can really Roll with the punches. He's kind and funny." Priscilla L. Vail, School Success Network.

- Six-year-old Kelly's mother wrote:

  "She's in first grade and is definitely 'overplaced.' I came to that conclusion very early in the school year. Along with her teacher we decided that Kelly would repeat first grade. Many children in her class are one full year older than she is chronologically.

  "I have had a gut feeling that Kelly wasn't ready for school, since she was 3-1/2 years old and entering nursery school. Her symptoms were classic. She continued to suck her thumb and have her special blanket up until she was 5-1/2 years old. She cried most of the time when I dropped her off at school and in kindergarten she stayed by my side until the teacher came to get her. Socially, Kelly was very immature.

  "I wanted my daughter to be out playing and having fun with the other children but this didn't happen. When she did play it was one-to-one.

  "Why then did I send her on? Not to place the blame on anyone because I know that it was my husband's and my decision that placed her. But I listened to her nursery school teacher and then again to her kindergarten teacher; they both felt she was ready to conquer the next grade up. My instinct all along was that my beautiful child needed a growth year. Back to the present, I get relief from my guilt now by knowing that Kelly does enjoy school this year. Since it was decided early in the year that she would repeat first grade, very little pressure was placed on her academically. She does receive remedial reading, but in a group of three and in her regular classroom. She brings home many incomplete papers and many marked wrong, but we ignore these (most of the time) and praise her on the ones she did well on. She has begun to play in groups and actually brings home friends from school.

"I am very grateful to her teacher for bringing this to a head at the beginning of the school year. We felt that to re-place Kelly in kindergarten after having her start first grade would be more detrimental to her already low self-image. So without the pressure to perform, Kelly has enjoyed her first full year in school."

- The mother of a boy who repeated kindergarten wrote of their experience:

  "When the kindergarten teacher first told me Scott needed extra time, I thought she was crazy. Gradually I began to realize she had his best interests at heart and it was my own insecurities that stopped me from seeing what she was talking about.

"Scott picked up some of my initial negative feelings, but once I assured him that it was a good thing and that he would be helping the teacher with the new children, he was just fine.

"I've been asked if he was traumatized. Not at all. As a matter of fact I believe the opposite is true. Had I pushed him ahead I think I would probably have problems with him now.

"When your child is bright, I imagine any parent, at first, has a hard time with the idea of repeating kindergarten, as I did. But now I see it as an opportunity. And I am just very grateful to his teacher for caring enough and being brave enough to go up against parents like me every year so that these children can get the time they need."

CHAPTER 10
How To Give A Child Support

"Most children are resilient and adaptable and can adapt to many demands that are made of them if they have the support of those who matter to them." *Kaczkowski, H. and Patterson, C.H. Counseling And Psychology In Elementary Schools.*

I cannot emphasize enough that for re-placement to be successful, it must be the result of a decision-making triangle—the school, the parents and the child. The school needs to support the decision and be ready to help make it work. Both parents need to understand and want this second chance for their child. Equally important, the child must be willing to give it a try.

Children need to understand why re-placement is recommended and what to expect. They should have some say in whatever options are available for an extra year in the grade. Usually children have strong feelings either about staying with the same teacher or having a different teacher. Changing schools is another option that might be important to some children.

Listening to their ideas and respecting their opinions helps children feel they have some control over their own lives. Understanding what worries or concerns them enables you both to develop strategies to cope with your child's fears of being teased or having to make new friends. Children need support in making this important change in their lives.

Children need support in making this important change in their lives.

Before The Issue Of Re-placement Comes Up

In school take time to listen to the child's feelings that are articulated and others that may be hidden behind defensive words. Acknowledge these feelings without being critical, judgmental or even *helpful*.

At home, if your child comes storming into the house after school screaming, "I hate school," this is not the time to pin her down and analyze why she hates school. An answer like "It sounds as if you had a rough day" is less likely to make her put up her defenses. Your child is feeling bad at the moment and what she needs most is the reassurance that you care. Knowing that you care is critical to your child now that a change is expected of her, even when it promises to be for the better. At this time your child needs unconditional love and support.

When parents are called to school for a conference, they shouldn't keep it a secret from the child. They should give their child a chance to list questions to ask the teacher. Even though the child might not be directly involved with this first conference, let him know that his input is valued.

Agreement among the adults involved is vital even though it isn't always easy.

In a child's world, when frustration and school failure erode her self-confidence and self-esteem, she frequently feels totally powerless to change or improve her life. Since adults hold the power in the eyes of the child, you must be sensitive to re-empowering the child if re-placement is to be successful.

When Teacher And Parents Agree That Re-placement Will Help

Agreement among the adults involved is vital even though it isn't always easy. But, in any event, disagreement needs to be thought through, negotiated and cleared up before re-placement can be considered a positive option.

Disagreement between parents, or between the parents and the school, puts the success of re-placement at risk. Children are very perceptive and will sense the tension between the adults, which only reinforces negative feelings about repeating a grade. Disharmony makes it harder for the child to develop positive feelings so necessary for a successful experience.

All the adults in a child's life need to pull in the same direction for re-placement to work effectively. When agreement abounds the child senses considerable support. Under these circumstances there is much to be gained from having the child be part of subsequent parent/teacher conferences. For one, it is reassuring for the child to witness his parents and teacher philosophically on the same side of the table. This adds immensely to a child's safety net.

A child's emotional reaction to being retained depends largely on how parents break the news.

INTRODUCING THE IDEA OF RE-PLACEMENT

"A child's emotional reaction to being retained depends largely on how parents break the news."
Louise Bates Ames, Ph.D.

How parents tell their child that they want him to repeat a grade will of course vary with the particulars of the situation. But several things are important to remember:

1) You need to first think through your own feelings about re-placement.

2) You need to be ready to listen to how your child feels about the possibility of re-placement.

3) You need to accept your child's overplacement as your oversight.

All adults who are going to talk with children about re-placement need to first think through their own disappointment and frustration. You need to work through some of the guilt, disappointment and anguish you might feel. It's important that you separate your own feelings from the child and her feelings. Without this, your feelings can often get in the way of talking with the child.

The next order of business is to listen to how a child feels about the possibility of repeating a grade. What does staying back mean to him? How does the child see himself? What worries him?

The child, for example, very often sees herself as dumb or stupid. Unfortunately, at this point in the child's life, everything confirms this. Be very careful not to deny this self-image. What seems a reassuring "But, you're not stupid," is really saying to the child that you are brushing off this deep concern as being something inconsequential—you just don't understand. Listen and accept the self-image with an acknowledgement like, "It must be miserable to feel that way." By accepting this negative self-image you have a better chance of helping the child compare it with how she might feel next year when she will be able to do the work.

If a child is in the wrong grade, it was a miscalculation that the parents and the school made inadvertently. Nonetheless it was a mistake and it is important for the child to know the adults in his world accept it as their mistake and not his. No young child is ever at fault for repeating a grade. A child in the wrong grade is a victim of circumstance and is not to blame.

But children usually do feel they are to blame. If they are not doing well in school, they feel they've let down their parents and teacher. As their school problems grow, most dialogue about their problems only reinforces this sense of being at fault. Therefore, parents need to make a special effort to absolve the child of all blame.

Parents, in particular, need to make a conscious effort to absolve the child of all blame.

What Parents Might Say

Let's take the case where parents are explaining to their child that they feel he should have another year in first grade before going on to second.

"We spoke with your teacher about how unhappy you seem to be with some things at school. She mentioned that you have trouble getting your work done and you sometimes cry when asked to do very hard work. She also said you have a hard time staying in your seat and that you would rather be outside playing.

"We told her you came home tired and cranky and we feel badly because sometimes you don't like school and feel it is too hard. We told her how you worry about school. We wondered why school seemed hard for a smart boy like you.

"Your teacher said she thought maybe the work

in first grade is too hard for you because you are just too young to do it. Toward the end of kindergarten last year, we noticed you becoming unhappy with school. Mom and Dad thought about having you stay in kindergarten another year. We think we made a mistake when we put you into first grade when you weren't finished growing yet.

"We started you in school too early and this is why you are having trouble with your school work now. If we had known how unhappy you were going to be in first grade, you could have stayed with your kindergarten teacher one more year.

"We made a mistake that needs to be corrected and we need your help to do it. We would like you to stay in first grade for another year. The work will be easier for you next year and you will be happier."

How Do Children React

Younger children who feel less peer pressure may feel some disappointment, but just as often they feel a great sense of relief that the struggle is over. For them the release of all that negative stress can be exhilarating. Freedom from school tension totally changes some children. One mother remarked that it was as if "her old child had been returned to her."

Other young children may be more matter-of-fact and simply take it in stride. Some children want to have the same teacher "next year." Others might want to have a different teacher. Because it is not unusual for overplaced children to have younger friends, they may want to be in the same room as a younger friend. But, on the other hand, they might not want to be in the same room as a younger brother or sister.

The potential damage of forced re-placement will outweigh any benefits it might bring.

Expect some young children to protest having to stay back. Don't expect or ask for an instant assent from them. If there is hesitation or real resistance, give the child a chance to think about any other options that might be possible.

If a child cannot be reassured about repeating a year, don't force re-placement on the child. The potential damage of forced re-placement will outweigh any benefits it might bring.

The reaction of older children is usually quite different from that of younger ones. An older child might feel devastated by the idea of losing his friends. If a child feels secure in his group, the risk of losing that status could outweigh any promise that correcting his grade placement will help him to succeed in school.

Peer pressure is also much greater in the upper elementary grades and children are very aware of the need to fit into the group. The need for peer approval puts the child in a painful dilemma.

Older children who are willing to try re-placement are keenly aware of whether or not they will be comfortable with a teacher. Again, some children want to stay with the same teacher while others want to be *promoted* to another teacher in the same grade. Some children would be far more comfortable repeating a grade if they could go to another school in the district or to private school. These options should be seriously explored. When a child feels strongly in favor of a new setting, try to find a way to make this possible. It will be easier for her to accomplish the change.

When older children *dig in* and refuse to repeat a grade, the school and parents would do well to reconsider the situation and explore other options. The failure and isolation that re-placement means to them may so threaten their already endangered self-esteem that they become desperate. If children raise the prospect of doing something self-destructive such as running away, dropping out or even committing suicide if they are forced to repeat a grade, the prospects of re-placement being successful are slim. This is not a time for a battle of wills. Only harm will result from any child/parent power struggle. Promote the child and look for other options as listed in chapters six and seven.

Love And Reassurance Count For A Lot

The decision has been made. The school, the parents and the child have all decided that it would be worth repeating the grade. Hopes are high that the child will do much better in school and that his self-confidence will grow.

Usually this takes a while. But sometimes one sees a dramatic change immediately. As principal I was called in one day to a combined third/fourth grade. Half the room was grade three and half was grade four with an aisle right down the center. A few weeks into the year, I received a note from the fourth grade teacher asking me to come to her room right away. I did and she said "Look at that little girl over there, the new girl."

This child had been young when she had entered school in another town. I looked over at her and she was sitting there, a silent sufferer with tears streaming down her checks. I went over and asked, "What's the matter?" She said, "I can't do any of the work here, I feel stupid."

So I asked, "Who do you play with?" She pointed and said, "Those girls over there in the third grade."

"Well," I asked, "would you like to slide your desk over (nine tiles in that direction) and do the work that they're doing?" It's lucky I was agile and could jump back, in time. Her desk slid right across the room. She got rid of that fourth grade material. She began working with the third grade material and for the first time in years she was able to do what the teacher asked of her and soared to the top of the class. That little girl came from under a terrible cloud in the fourth grade over to the sunshine side of the room. We slid her desk nine tiles and changed her life!

Often, however, it takes time for a child to

regroup his energies and to transform his view of school and himself. The older the child, the longer the school misery, and the harder it can be for a child to believe things can really change.

What helps? Love, for one thing. Love demonstrated by hugs, a pat on the back, words of affection and appreciation—small, true, day-by-day signs that parents aren't disappointed, ashamed or angry.

Each experience of feeling competent and being observed as competent helps affirm the child's self-concept.

Both teachers and parents need to look for ways to pay special attention to things that the child does well. These don't need to be big things, but whenever the child does something competently, whether it is shooting a basket, setting the table, or watering the plants, take note of it. Let the child understand that you frequently see her as a competent person, rather than just *one big mess of problems.*

In the classroom, a child who is repeating the grade may well be a good tutor for some of the children just coming into the grade. Tutoring and being the one who already knows how to do something can give a big boost to a child's confidence. Each experience of feeling competent and being observed as competent helps affirm the child's self-concept. Rebuilding self-esteem takes time and nurturing.

Repeating a grade still means real work for the child. But this time there is a very good chance for accomplishment and a sense of mastery. Be realistic in your reassurance and do not take the position that *everything will now be okay.* The truth is that the child will work hard, see results and be pleased with what he can do.

Helping A Child Communicate Feelings

Communicating one's feelings in words is not always easy. Be alert to the messages and feelings that lie behind a child's words. Is there frustration, confusion or anguish that they don't know how to put into words? As children grow older, they often become more defensive, afraid of exposing themselves to criticism, ridicule or additional failure. The idea of discussing problems or feelings can be very threatening to them.

In some instances it helps the child to know that someone else has gone through the same thing and felt the same confusion. It can be helpful to share a story of another child who repeated a grade. *What Am I Doing In This Grade?* by Louise Bates Ames is a small illustrated book that you can use with first graders. Amusing illustrations and a lighthearted text look at the dilemma of John, who started school too soon. John repeats first grade and the story ends happily. Another book, *Staying Back,* by Janice Hale Hobby and Gabrielle and Daniel Rubin includes seven short stories about children of different ages who repeated a grade for various reasons. These stories describe how the children felt as they were struggling and how they felt after they repeated the grade. There are notes in the back of the book that suggest ways of using these stories to help children get in touch with their own feelings and express them.

HOW IT CAN BE AN OPPORTUNITY

Children may accept the decision to repeat a grade because it seems inevitable, the only choice, or for a number of other negative reasons. They may think that *things are always decided for them*. It is important for children to come to an understanding of why they are being re-placed. It is not enough for the adults in their world to tell them that it is *a second chance,* or *an opportunity to turn failure into success.*

Children, especially as they grow older, need help in reframing how they see themselves and their school experience. They also need a handy, acceptable explanation. They need something to tell friends and relatives and even themselves about why they are repeating a grade.

To help children come up with positive ideas about repeating a grade, start with how they see themselves and the problems they are having in school. Start, perhaps, with that self-image of being *dumb* or *stupid.* At an earlier stage you acknowledged that children feel this way. Now explore what makes them feel that way. "I can't read." "I'm no good at math." Or, the answer might be the defensive "I don't know." Explore the possibilities as to what would make them feel smarter. What if they could be a good reader, maybe the best in the class? What if they could be really good in math? What if they could do their homework faster, and there was more time to play outside? In exploring these wishes, these "what if's," you will find some goals that mean something in terms of their experience. You can help them find and articulate their own positive explanation. "I'm repeating second grade so that I'll be a really good reader."

One thing that sometimes helps is for children to do *before* and *after* pictures of themselves. *Before* is a chance to show and talk about what didn't go well; *after* is how that is going to change next year.

A School Support System

Barbara Davis, a teacher in Montgomery County, Maryland, has developed an effective support system for children who are repeating in the primary grades, which she calls GAC—"Getting Another Chance." In the spring, she calls a meeting for all the primary children in the school who will be repeating a grade in the fall. She also invites other children who have been retained in previous years. "They're key supporters," she writes, "because they're peers. They've been teased; they've felt not very smart and they've felt as if they've disappointed their parents and themselves." At the meeting everyone is invited to say how they feel. Those who have been retained talk first. They answer questions such as: How did you feel getting another chance? Were you scared? Happy? Why? Were you teased? How did you handle the teasing?

Misery thrives on misinformation, mystery, innuendos and the recycling of old school tales.

Then each of the children who were looking ahead to their *second chance* answer the same questions. If children are not ready to answer in turn, they get a second chance at that too. "So that they can verbally begin to acknowledge their situation and cope with their feelings."

"Bringing all these people together visually discloses the fact that the GAC children are not alone. They meet children they can talk to at school without fear of reprisal, and they meet adults who empathize with them." There is a follow-up meeting in the fall to re-establish the support system and to let the children know that there is help available if a problem arises that is too difficult for them to handle.

Talking About Re-placement With The Whole Class

Misery thrives on misinformation, mystery, innuendos and the recycling of old school tales. Having to repeat a grade should not become a shameful secret that gets gossiped about or whispered. There can be great benefit in having an open class discussion on grade re-placement. Open discussion reduces the age-old stigma of retention. There is no shame attached to something that has total open acceptance of everyone in the child's world.

Several years ago when I was teaching fifth grade, I was trying to help a young boy who had been re-placed to fourth grade. He was new to our school. His parents had brought him in on the first day. He was a very small fifth grader. The child was in my room for about three weeks and literally could not do what we were asking of fifth graders. He didn't recognize the material. He constantly took in-house field trips—always doing something in the room but never quite producing the work.

I called his parents to arrange a conference before school. I explained what it was that concerned me and the father turned to the mother and said "I told you it wouldn't work. She changed the birth certificate." The child had been born in January but they had moved the date up to December to meet the cut off date in the previous school system, to get him into school early.

We made the decision then and there that we would re-place him to fourth grade right away. Although he was willing, he also felt devastated.

I have always found it helpful to have a class discuss problems that come up, particularly when they deal with people's feelings. So when the class arrived that morning and finally settled down, I explained that the new boy was going back to be with the fourth graders for the rest of the year. Fifth grade work was just too hard for him and he was unhappy with it.

At that, one of the students jumped up and said, "Well, let's give him a *car wash*!" I hadn't thought about it, but a *car wash* was just what this little boy needed to help him feel better.

A *car wash* is a technique that I had introduced and used with the class several times when a child was upset and needed emotional support. We used it, for instance, with a girl who had seen a bus run over her puppy dog as she left for school. She arrived at school in a terrible state. There were plenty of sad, bad feelings that she needed help getting rid of—feelings to be *washed away*.

So the class formed into two facing lines and the girl walked between them. As she walked this friendly gauntlet, each of the *washers* said or did something they felt would make her feel better. She was given stickers, pencils, erasers and lots of supportive comments. One boy even offered to let her keep his dog for a week.

The ground rules for the *car wash* were always made clear to everyone: say something helpful, the kind of thing you would want said to you. After all, each of them knew that, someday, they themselves might need the *car wash*.

The little boy who was going back to fourth grade was crying and he clutched a kleenex as he walked through the *car wash*. I watched as kids spontaneously said things like "I took two years in first grade," "I went to the transition program before first grade." "I never started first grade until I was seven." One little girl said, "It's perfectly all right, we like you anyway." She was so enthused she reached out and gave him a kiss. He, of course, went *yuck*.

But let me tell you where the *rubber really hits the road* for the child. The last boy in line said, "Hey, we all play outside at the same time for recess. We're still going to be your friends and play with you. It's just that you're going to go to school in a different room." That was the remark that did the trick. He said "Good! I'm going back to fourth."

Repeating a grade is a tremendous change in a child's life. Change brings its own kind of anxiousness and however easy or hard it may seem for the child, he or she needs as much support as possible from all quarters.

Testimonies From Kids Who Have "Lived Through It"

- Justin, nine-years-old, who repeated second grade, wrote this book about it in third grade:

1. The first year.

My first year in second grade was hard for me because I was not ready for second grade. It was not because I was dumb, it was because I was not ready. So if you stay back, don't think you're dumb even if someone says you are. You're just not ready. My first year was hard for me because I couldn't figure out the work I got. I didn't want to go to school in the morning because I was afraid I'd get a lot of homework. I was also afraid that I would lose all my recess (30 minutes) and sit for the whole shebang. Then after recess we had lots of work to do (well, at least I did). But look at the bright side, you have another year to get better at your work.

2. Good news and bad news.

Well, the good news is that you will probably have better grades this year. The bad news is that all your friends are in third. But don't feel bad because you'll probably make new friends. I made new friends (better ones, too). So stick with the good ones, be smart. If you're smart you'll get A's and if you get A's you'll have a good, matter of fact, a great report card. So see what staying back can do for you. A lot, don't you think so? I do. So if you stay back don't feel bad, feel good and remember good news. So look at what staying back can do for you. A lot, don't you think?

3. The second year.

The second year was good for me because this time I was ready for second. I got my work done. I got to play at recess. So the second year was the best year for me and probably for you. The second year you learn more, get better grades, make new friends and play at recess instead of doing your work and you probably won't have a lot of homework. Now, that's the good news, don't you think? But there is some bad news. Some kids might call you names, but don't let that bother you because there's a lot more good news than bad news. So remember second year is best.

4. Where do I go from here?

Well, after your second year in any grade you'll probably ask that old question, where do I go from here, teacher? Well, where you go is the next grade, unless you're graduating. But when I was in second I would wonder where do I go from here. I found out to third. I am doing great in third and that is all because I stayed back. I feel good that I stayed back because I'm doing much, much better. Remember, staying back isn't bad. Actually, it's good for you, so remember this book and feel good about staying back."

- Brian T. Smith, a high school student in Titusville, Florida wrote this about his experience:

Eighth Grade Decision

"If anyone asked why I was repeating I would gladly inform them that it was my own free choice. I was born in December and entered kindergarten four years later under the pretense that I would be turning five in a couple of months. But, apparently, those months were needed for me to mature and fit in with the rest of the students my age.

"I had no problems academically, immediately receiving the highest scores possible. But I didn't have any friends my age. In fourth grade I went from straight A's to F's and developed the title of class clown. Although my parents punished me, excessively, my grades and conduct only improved a little.

"Everyday, after school, I would come home crying. I would retreat to my bedroom, complaining that no one cared about me. My parents began to worry and started taking me to a psychiatrist once a week. Convinced that this was my natural behavior, the psychiatrist told my parents that this was how I would remain...they refused to believe this.

"Then one day, my mother asked if I would go to a meeting with her. Reluctantly, I agreed to go to this educational program on developmental placement. The program was created primarily for students four to six years old, but when my mother went she found it was applicable for all ages. After listening to a speaker on how common my problem was, I knew that this was the right solution for me. So I enrolled into eighth grade at Madison Middle School.

"No one tried to influence my decision in any way and left my future up to me. If I had been told that I was to stay back a year, I would never have agreed to do so. This way, I made my own decision and was able to stick to it, besides.

"Now, I look back at my life and wonder what would have happened if I hadn't decided to repeat eighth grade. But I know, no matter what would have occurred, I would have never been as happy as I am now, and thankful for the many friends I have acquired since then."

Brian is now in the National Honor Society, Who's Who Among High School Students two years running, won writing contests in school, and is active in the Anchor Club, theatre arts, and many other school and out-of-school activities.

- Waldo Jones, Head of Lower School, Rippowam-Cisqua School, Bedford, New York has received these reactions from children who have been re-placed:

Girl who repeated fourth grade:

"Everything, even at home, got much better after I took another year in fourth grade."

Boy who repeated kindergarten:

"School is great—just great! I just know I can do the work."

Boy who repeated third grade:

"Last year in third grade I was just sort of there. I wasn't much of anyone. This year I was a candidate for class office—no problem—and guess what? I was elected! In sports too, I got to be Captain. This has been awesome!"

An eight-year-old girl who earlier had repeated pre-kindergarten:

"That was a long time ago, but I can remember my Mom crying and calling Grandma after her conference with my teacher. It was such a big deal to Mom. She called it The Big Decision and talked about it to all her friends. I really didn't understand or care much which room I was in."

Boy who repeated second grade:

"It didn't even seem like the same school my second year in second grade. It seemed so much friendlier."

- Jason Smith, eleven years old wrote:

Little Late

I came into the world later than expected
walked at one,
read at four.
At three I learned to open a door.
I started school way too early—
because I'm a little late.

K, 1, and 2 were fairly easy,
I understood.
I learned.
Along came third—I hit a snag.
And fourth was such a drag—
because I'm a little late.

It took two years to do my fifth.
I grew
and I matured.
My first was OK and my second was terrific.
It is not a deadly fate—
Now I'm not a little late.

CHAPTER 11
Questions Teachers Ask About Re-placement

Q. Should I repeat a child when the parents are opposed?
A. No! Never repeat a child against the parents' wishes. It simply will not work. Parental support is crucial to the success of a re-placement. Parents must have the final say.

Q. I know if I promote this child, he will surely fail, but I can't convince the parents to let me keep him another year. What should I do?
A. Promote the child, recommend remediation to help the child compensate, and continue working with the parents. Remember, parents must be allowed to make their own decisions. Parents who refuse at first often come around to the teacher's recommendation after witnessing their child's continuing struggle.

Q. How early into the school year should I inform

parents that their child is struggling and might need to take two years to complete the program?
A. Alert parents at the earliest possible moment. While some parents argue that your early prediction doesn't give their child a fair chance, most parents appreciate being notified at the first sign of trouble. Teachers have a moral obligation to always act in the child's best interest. If the child is experiencing school difficulty, alert the parents immediately so you can chart a suitable course of action.

Q. I have a child who has struggled all year in the wrong grade. He is able to do just enough to get by, and has been passed along from grade to grade. Should I promote him on trial?
A. No. If you have enough information to promote a child on trial, condition or probation, then you have enough information to re-place the child to the correct grade. Don't be a party to amortizing school failure over a period of years. Give the child a second chance now!

Q. A second grader in my room has a low IQ and his work reflects his ability. Will repeating this child increase his level of work?
A. It is doubtful. Repeating a grade will not change a child's IQ but may make him more comfortable by reducing the stress. This child might benefit more from being tutored or receiving special remedial help or being put into a class with fewer children.

Q. I suspect that a student of mine is learning disabled. Should I repeat the child and wait for improvements?
A. No. Simply repeating a child will not change the child's learning disability. Waiting the year might serve to delay an evaluation by one year and, therefore, postpone badly needed special services. However, if a child is both young and learning disabled, the child might benefit from both special services and an extra year to complete a grade.

Q. What kind of documentation should I have before I recommend re-placement?
A. Document specific areas of difficulty such as a child's:

- ability to stay on task, focus and complete it.
- level of frustration indicated by crying, tantrums, depression, etc.

You can also gather helpful information from individually administered tests. You can present parent/teacher observation of stress signs and signals anecdotally. These observations, by the way, prove to be highly predictive of school success or difficulty.

Q. A parent wants her child to repeat and I disagree. The child can do average work if he applies himself. I don't see the same problems as the parent sees. She claims her child has reverted to bed wetting, morning headaches and stomach aches, and constant complaints of hating school. What should I do about this stalemate?

A. Parents are very perceptive concerning how their child feels about school. Many children are compliant, *good* children at school, but really only go through the motions. It is not at all unusual for a child like this to fall apart at home. The child is probably *indicating* at home the degree of school stress. Listen to this parent carefully because she might see a need very different from what you see.

Q. My principal will not allow me to repeat any students because of some articles that she has read. What do I do?

A. Some decision makers may only know children through reading journals and, unfortunately, that's not the real world. Your base of *real life* experience gives you a very different view. There are several things you can do. Ask your administrator to read the following publications:

Is Your Child In The Wrong Grade?

I Hate School

What Am I Doing In This Grade?

Staying Back

Stop School Failure

Summer Children

Changing To A Developmentally Appropriate Curriculum, Successfully

Dialogues On Developmental
Curriculum

These books will provide a good basis for discussion and should serve to put you both on the same track. After this, you might want to invite your administrator to visit your classroom and experience all that she's just read. Your administrator wants to do what is right for children and should be able to come to an understanding about the plight of children in the wrong grade.

Q. Should I repeat a child who has already had an extra year of time?
A. No. If children need more than one year of extra time then there are probably other issues influencing their performance such as low IQ, learning disabilities, emotional problems, or physical ailments. Special services or programs are usually recommended for these children. There are a few cases, however, where a second year proves beneficial. Extreme caution is urged in selecting such students.

Q. Why is the available research on retention negative?
A. Because most of the retention research has been conducted on children who are low achievers due to low IQ's, emotional problems, or learning disabilities. In these cases the research is accurate in stating that these children do not fare much better the second year in the same grade. As a matter of

fact, some do even worse the second year. A developmentally young, overplaced child is not the same as a child in the above groups and should not be categorized as such. But unfortunately they are, and hence become misrepresented in the negative research on retention. Basically we should be repeating those children who are developmentally immature and overplaced.

Q. Our school staff is divided on who and how many school officials should attend a teacher/parent conference on re- placement. Is there one answer?
A. Think in terms of a decision-making triangle—Child-Teacher- Parents. Too many school officials might overwhelm parents or intimidate them into making a decision they are uncomfortable with. On the other hand, a second or potentially difficult conference might warrant the presence of the principal or school psychologist. A third party sometimes facilitates the decision- making process.

Q. I read an article recently stating that a transition year is a retention. How can this be?
A. That statement is only true in the eyes of the writer! Retention is repeating the same grade. Transition is an additional full grade or program between two existing grades—i.e., pre-first is a grade between kindergarten and first grade for those children who are chronologically six, but developmentally young. Transition is developmental progression.

Q. The behavior of an emotionally disturbed child in my class has greatly limited his ability to keep up with his work. Will re-placement help?
A. Only if wrong grade placement is the root of the problem. Repeating a grade will not change the condition of an emotionally disturbed child. The needs of this child would be better served by a special program.

Q. When can re-placement be harmful to a child?
A. When the wrong student is elected for re-placement. It is not recommended that teachers retain those students who are:

- emotionally disturbed
- learning disabled (unless they are also developmentally young)
- long-time school failures
- low IQ
- slow learners
- those children whose parents are against it.

Other alternatives would better serve the needs of these students. See chapters six and seven.

CHAPTER 12

Questions Parents Ask About Re-placement

Q. Isn't it always the *slow* child who is kept back?

A. No. Some very bright children need an extra year of time. For some children, the easiest part of school is the academic work, but school success requires more than academic achievement. For instance, if a child "always has her head in a book," and doesn't have time or energy left for social, physical, and emotional development to match the intellectual side, that child is not happy. When children are sent to school before they are ready, they are likely to become *bookworms, teacher-pleasers,* or *class clowns* rather than risk being themselves.

Q. Our first grader is a poor student and we believe it is simply because she is immature. We are reluctant to repeat her because she is taller than most of her classmates. Should she stay back?

A. Most parents would rather have a large, successful child than a large, unsuccessful one! In reality, physically larger and older children often become the class leaders. Ask yourself if it's better for your daughter to experience momentary embarrassment than endure years of humiliation and shame because she feels inadequate and stupid?

Q. Is it ever too late to repeat a grade?
A. It depends on the child. Many children gain immediate relief from the stress of being in the wrong grade. On the other hand, if an older child has experienced a long history of school failure, the damage may be too great to undo proper grade placement.

The most important factor to consider is your child's attitude toward staying back. How would your child handle it? How would you handle it? Don't forget...your child's attitude is usually directly influenced by your reaction!

Q. Can a child move back a grade once school has started?
A. Yes! If a child is unhappy in school and is struggling to keep up, it makes good sense to intervene and start the correct program now, not in three months or three years when the child has experienced an overdose of school failure. The earlier, the better!

Q. Is social promotion recommended once a child is beyond the primary grades?

A. Social promotion, the automatic promotion of all children up through the grades, was probably invented to avoid confrontations with parents. Social promotion was meant to protect children from feeling rotten about themselves. However, it achieves the opposite result. Instead of protecting them, children continue to feel inadequate and helpless when they cannot do the work the teacher gives them. Remaining in programs where they cannot succeed, through no fault of their own, keeps children from the possibility of ever achieving success.

Q. At a parent conference in November (just nine weeks into the school year!) we were told that our child was a candidate for repeating the grade. Is it possible for a teacher to know in just nine weeks?
A. Yes. Most experienced teachers know or at least suspect almost immediately when your child is at risk. Remember, teachers are professionals who are trained in observing child behavior and who have years of experience as accurate predictors of school success or failure. It is also the teacher's professional obligation to alert you as early as possible of any positive or negative behavior your child might express.

Q. My daughter's teacher told us she has a *gut feeling* our child should stay back. She is doing almost average work. Is a *gut feeling* reliable?
A. I prefer calling it teacher judgment based on an intuitive sense. Teacher observation is highly pre-

dictive of school success. Listen to your child's teacher. It pays to keep an open ear and listen to your own intuitive feelings as well.

Q. What about the *stigma* associated with staying back?

A. Years ago it was shameful for a child to *stay back*. The child was considered *stupid* or *slow*. Children felt guilty, parents felt guilty, everyone felt that something was inherently wrong with them.

Today there is a better name for staying back. It is *grade re-placement*. Today many children take an extra year of time because we recognize that all children are developmentally distinct individuals who require varied amounts of time to complete the curriculum. The possible *stigma* is an adult issue unless, of course, parents mistakenly pass that idea along to their children.

Q. Will my child have to repeat all the work, even the work he knows?

A. When your child repeats a grade, he will usually start where he left off the previous year. He has *gone through the motions* the first time, but will really understand the material the second time. I've heard many children say, "I like doing some of the same work again. I feel so smart!"

Q. My husband is dead set against our son repeating. He himself repeated a grade and he doesn't want that to happen to his son. We are in a real dilemma.

A. Parents' past experiences greatly influence their perceptions. You would be wise to have a third party help to negotiate your differences. It should be someone who can help your husband understand how differently re-placement is viewed and handled in school today. There are also reading recommendations in the bibliography.

Q. What will our friends and our child's grandparents say when they find out that our child is being re-placed?
A. The neighbors may have plenty of comments, some supportive and some not so helpful. Remember, many well-intentioned people might be quick with opinions, but have not lived with and worried over a child who is struggling and miserable in school.

Grandparents are another story. They are emotionally involved and care deeply. Recognize and respect their feelings of hurt, disappointment and embarrassment. Remember, too, that when they attended school, the usual reason children stayed back was because they were perceived as *lazy* or *stupid*. They will need time and information to help them understand that re-placement is a positive move in their grandchild's best interest.

Q. I suspect my child needs another year in the same grade. What should I do?
A. Number one, trust your instincts! You know your child better than anyone else. And do make

certain that you and your spouse share the same viewpoint. Secondly, review your child's school history by meeting with teachers. Also, review in your own mind how your child has reacted to school, past and present. Thirdly, read literature on the subject of school readiness and developmental education. And fourth, have your child assessed to validate developmental age level for correct grade placement.

Collectively, these steps will help confirm your intuitive feelings about your child's grade placement. Remember, waiting will not harm your child, but pushing will.

Q. My son's teacher does not want to repeat our child. My husband and I want it. What do we do now?

A. It is not uncommon to find parents and a teacher taking opposite positions on the subject of grade re-placement. Try first to determine exactly why the teacher opposes it. If the teacher does not favor retention under any circumstances or if you disagree with her reasons and both you and your husband are fully convinced that your child will benefit from grade re-placement, settle for nothing less. This firm stand may cause the parent/school relationship to be strained and may warrant the child being reassigned to another class or school.

Q. The principal wants to repeat my daughter. Isn't it unusual for girls to repeat?

A. No, although more boys than girls tend to be developmentally young. Girls, though developmentally young, are frequently overlooked and inadvertently placed in the wrong grade.

Q. If my child is reading on grade level, why is the teacher suggesting she repeat a grade?
A. Academic performance is only one area to consider. A child's social, emotional and physical needs should be of primary concern as well. Many children have good reading skills, but may be immature socially, emotionally or physically. In this situation reading is considered a splinter skill. Children are often passed from grade to grade based on their ability to read, but this skill might not be enough to sustain them at grade level if they are immature in other areas.

Q. Will my child be emotionally damaged by repeating a grade?
A. I have yet to see a child who is developmentally young be emotionally damaged by being re-placed into the right grade. Emotional damage is more likely to occur from not being properly placed. Most children repeating a grade experience emotional upset to some degree at first as they try to sort out what is happening to them. This short period of anxiety is common in any important change.

There is the possibility of emotional damage, however, if the child has been overplaced for a number of years and never repeated. The risk depends on the particular child and situation. Given a choice, I would opt for the temporary upset that might accompany early grade re-placement over the damage associated with long-term overplacement.

Q. Will my child's self-concept and self-esteem be affected by repeating a grade?
A. Much depends on your child's temperament and your attitude. Many children express tremendous relief and skyrocket in their studies and self-esteem as a result of being in a grade that fits them.

Daily struggles with school can erode your child's self-value. Child development experts are quick to agree that once self-esteem is tainted or gone, it is difficult to recover. It is important to nurture self-confidence by correcting wrong grade placement before too much damage is done. The earlier, the better. Many educators contend that repeating a grade is less harmful than continuing down a path of school failure and misery. Remember, school failure hurts for a long, long time.

Q. Our kindergarten son is very bright, but very young. He knows how to do his school work but never quite completes it. If he repeats the same grade, won't he be bored?
A. On the contrary, your child will find his work very rewarding and enjoyable when he can complete all assigned tasks. The very young child often finds it difficult to stay still for very long, is off-task,

inattentive, and easily bored if asked to do something he is not ready for. Next year when your child is more mature, developmentally ready, he will possess self-motivation, self-stimulation, and self-control, the necessary ingredients for a successful learning experience.

Q. If my child repeats, will it matter that he is a year older?
A. Children do not seem as concerned about chronological age as adults are. Many children report that they like being a year older. It isn't uncommon to find a three-year age span in any given classroom.

Q. If my son stays back, he will be in his sister's grade. Is that alright?
A. It is usually advisable to have siblings assigned to separate rooms. An important factor will be the degree of sibling rivalry and competition. Some degree is normal, of course, but if re-placement is also threatening his *position* in the family, seek the help of a counselor to assist your family as a whole with this problem.

Q. My husband wants to *red-shirt* our son. Will this hurt him later on?
A. *Red-shirting*, giving a boy an extra year, usually in junior high, so that he will be physically more mature in athletic competition, has been popular with fathers for decades. Parent enthusiasm seems

to be a major factor in making it acceptable to the child.

Q. Will my child make new friends easily?
A. Most children have a propensity for making new friends. Most are adaptable and will readily adjust to a new peer group. As adults, we see this, but that doesn't make a child's anxiety about making new friends any less real. This is usually your child's number one fear about re-placement. Take it seriously and help your child think up strategies that he can use to make new friends.

Q. How will my child's friends react to his repeating a grade?
A. Your child's friends and siblings deserve an explanation. Part of coming to a decision with your child should be a simple statement about why she is repeating—something she can use to explain it to friends and relatives. You might also want to take an opportunity to talk about it with some of your child's close friends. Explain why you feel it is going to help her to spend another year in the same grade. Engage their support and ideas about things like friends and teasing. Most children will surprise you with how much they understand what a friend needs.

Q. My child has a learning disability. He receives help in a special class each day. In addition to his disability he is developmentally young. Will repeating help my child?

A. The general rule is not to repeat a child whose school difficulty stems from an identifiable learning disability. If you feel that he is both developmentally young and learning disabled and that he is uncomfortable in his present grade placement, discuss the possibility with his teacher and the other specialists who have set up his program. But only decide on re-placement if your child favors the idea.

CHAPTER 13
Questions Children Ask About Re-placement

Q. Should I have the same teacher or a new one?
A. That decision is up to you. If you worked well with your last year's teacher, you might want to have her again next year. She knows what work you have completed and where you left off at the end of the year.

Some boys and girls like having a new teacher whose program is very different from the year before so it's a new experience. You need to be with the teacher who makes you comfortable.

Q. Will I do well next year if I stay back?
A. Yes. If you stay back you will have time you need to complete your work. You won't feel so rushed. Most boys and girls like having a second chance to complete a grade they haven't finished.

Q. Will my mom and dad think I'm bad if I stay back?

A. No. Your parents know you are a good boy. They fully support having you take two years to complete a grade. They only want you to be happy in school.

Q. Will people think I'm stupid if I stay back?
A. Today most people know that many children start school in the wrong grade. They also know that in order to correct a wrong assignment, you will need to take two years to complete your present grade. This is considered normal.

Q. Will my friends tease me for staying back?
A. Yes, undoubtedly some children will tease you as they might tease a person for falling down, having freckles or speaking a different language. Many times they don't intend to be mean, it's just that they are sometimes not very thoughtful of someone else's feelings. If the taunting persists, your parents should ask your teacher to help.

Q. Will I have to repeat the work I already completed?
A. No. You will pick up where you left off last year. Wherever you left off in June is where you will start in September.

Additional Reading

Better Late Than Early
A New Approach to Your Child's Education
Dorothy N. Moore, Raymond S. Moore
New York, New York: Reader's Digest Press, 1977
236 pages paperback

This book contains vital information for parents who are faced with growing pressures to start their children in school at younger and younger ages. The Moores support with careful research the message that the trend toward early academics is not only misguided but harmful. Sections on the legalities of school readiness, child development and attachment, and the parents' role in school entrance give complete, carefully documented information.

Child Behavior
Specific Advice on Problems of Child Behavior
Frances L. Ilg, M.D., Louise Bates Ames, Ph.D., Sidney M. Baker, M.D.
New York, New York: Harper Rowe, 1981
360 pages paperback

From the Gesell Institute of Human Development comes this comprehensive book on child behavior. The information presented is based on the fact that individual behaviors develop predictably and that each age has patterned, predictable characteristics. With this understanding Ames, Ilg and Baker address specific behavior problems related to eating, sleeping and dreams, tensional outlets, children's fears, and many other areas. Further sections on the parent-child relationship, school success, behavior illness and diagnostic testing complete this very informative volume. While it is easy to read and not overly technical, Child Behavior is a thorough treatment of a very broad subject.

The Difficult Child
Dr. Stanley Turecki and Leslie Tonner
New York, New York: Bantam Books, 1985
240 pages paperback

A good discussion of how to help children change inappropriate behavior.

I Hate School
Some Common Sense Answers for Parents Who Wonder Why.
Including The Sign and Signals of the Overplaced Child.
Jim Grant
Rosemont, New Jersey: Programs for Education 1986
115 pages paperback

With humor, wisdom and great insight Jim Grant takes a look at the reasons some children hate school. While this is a relatively short paperback and can be read quickly, it contains case studies, theory and research to show that overplaced children—those who are in the wrong grade—are set up to fail. As an important bonus, I Hate School has a section entitled "Signs and Signals of the Overplaced Child." No parent or educator should be without this information.

Is Your Child In The Wrong Grade?
Louise Bates Ames, Ph.D.
Rosemont, New Jersey: Modern Learning Press, 1978
151 pages paperback

In a voice similar to the one she uses in face-to-face meetings with parents concerned about their children's school success, Dr. Ames writes about correct grade placement. This book is a must for parents—it is specific, complete and based on sound research by The Gesell Institute of Human Development. Dr. Ames bases her work on children's developmental stages and covers what constitutes correct placement, developmental placement assessments, recognizing unreadiness and overplacement. She concludes with a question and answer section that will be helpful to all parents and educators concerned with school success.

Miseducation
Preschoolers at Risk
David Elkind
New York, New York: Alfred A. Knopf, 1987
221 pages hardcover

Dr. David Elkind, author of The Hurried Child and All Grown Up And No Place To Go, has written this book as an important warning to parents. Current trends to hurry preschool children in academics and athletics in the interest of producing superkids are putting children at needless risk psychologically and physically. This book explores the "earlier-is-better" myth and studies the results of proper and improper programs for young children. Elkind also looked at the impact of miseducation on self-esteem. Finally, he presents an important section on what parents should look for when considering preschool programs, kindergarten and private educational systems. This is a carefully written, well documented, enlightening and somewhat alarming study done in Elkind's smooth, readable style.

No Easy Answers:
The Learning Disabled Child at Home and at School
Sally L. Smith
New York, New York: Bantam Books, 1980
326 pages paperback

Learning disability specialist Sally L. Smith has given parents and teachers a sensitive, detailed and even comforting book on how to recognize and deal with learning disabilities in children. For every teacher or parent who has been frustrated, mystified or angry about these hidden handicaps, she gives information on possible causes and the often difficult solutions. The overall tone is encouraging and while there is a great deal of material presented in one volume, it reads quickly and easily. It includes sections on teachers' concerns and feelings, teaching through the arts, public law, testing and goals and objectives.

One Piece Of The Puzzle
Barbara Carll and Nancy Richard
Rosemont, New Jersey: Programs for Education
77 pages paperback

A wonderfully practical manual for implementing a school readiness program.

Questions Parents Ask
Louise Bates Ames, Ph.D.
New York, New York: Clarkson N. Potter, Inc., 1988
286 pages paperback

The parent who picks up this latest book by Dr. Ames will find it difficult to put down. Every question (or certainly most) about child growth, development and behavior seems to be here. Only someone as astute as Dr. Ames could address so many questions as effectively. Included are 30 major topics from school readiness to sibling relationships to sleep problems. Questions are answered with insight, humor, compassion and wisdom; they make this book a must for parents, and the difficult job of child rearing a little easier.

Smart Kids With School Problems
Things to Know and Ways to Help
Priscilla Vail
New York, New York: E. P. Dutton, 1989
256 pages hardcover

Parents and teachers will both find this book valuable in understanding and working with these challenging "Conundrum Kids".

Staying Back
Janice Hale Hobby with Gabrielle and Daniel Rubin
Gainsville, Florida: Triad Publishing Company, 1982
93 pages paperback

For every child who has ever been anxious about staying back, for every parent concerned about his child's experience, and for the teacher of these children, here is a sensitive, simple book. From emotional issues to technicalities of repeating, author Janice Hale Hobby shows us what children go through. Studies of seven children who succeed because of proper handling of their problems make encouraging reading for all ages.

Stop School Failure
Louise Bates Ames, Ph.D., Clyde Gillespie and John W. Streff
Rosemont, New Jersey: Programs for Education, 1985
193 pages hardcover

Written for parents, this book also belongs in the hands of educators and administrators as it helps each group to understand the problems children face in school The authors, all from The Gesell Institute of Human Development, look at the causes of and solutions for school failure. Parents will get vital information from case studies of six children who are experiencing school failure. In addition to sections on child development, you will find information on vision, reading problems and schools of the future. Stop School Failure explores the important issues in a thorough, helpful manner.

Summer Children
Ready or Not for School
James K. Uphoff, June E. Gilmore, Rosemarie Huber
Middletown, Ohio: J & J Publishing Company, 1986
114 pages paperback

The authors of this book say "We feel, on the basis of the research we have done and after reviewing data provided by others, that we are tempted to say that every child under the age of five years, six months should wait a year before starting kindergarten." Summer Children looks at several different types of children and their degree of readiness for school, and presents a wealth of information and important research findings to help parents and educators start children in school at the correct time.

Superimmunity For Kids
Leo Galland and Dian Buchman
New York, New York: Doubleday & Company. Inc., 1989
400 pages hardcover

The first truly scientific, stage-by-stage guide to maximum health through nutrition, for children from infancy through adolescence. A book that looks at the various kinds of behavior problems that are triggered by allergies and biochemical hypersensitivity, and discusses how to treat them nutritionally.

What Am I Doing In This Grade?
Louise Bates Ames, Ph.D.
Rosemont, New Jersey: Programs for Education, 1985
31 pages paperback

"How come I'm always falling asleep in school? Maybe I'm not ready for all this. I wasn't even five when I started school this fall..." So speaks John, a kindergartner who started school at 4 years and 9 months of age. This lighthearted yet important book can be read very quickly and speaks of the problems encountered by children who start school too soon. The ending is a happy one as John takes some special tests and repeats first grade. Here is a book for teachers, parents and children who are dealing with John's problems. Delightful illustrations complete Dr. Ames' book, making it not only important but a pleasure to read.

Your Child's Growing Mind
A Guide to Learning and Brain Development from Birth to Adolescence.
Jane M. Healy, Ph.D.
New York, New York: Doubleday, 1987
324 pages hardcover

This sane and readable guide by a neuropsychologist, who is also a teacher, parent and learning specialist, is invaluable for parents and professionals alike.

Glossary

Academic Retention: Grade repetition based on a child's lack of academic skills acquisition.

Developmental Age: The age at which a child is behaving as a total organism—a functioning age. A child might be functioning at an average or above average level intellectually or in other aspects of his development, but a composite of his whole development might place him at a younger functioning age. Developmental age is the age where a child can sustain, where the child is "grounded."

Developmental Education: Curriculum and concepts that are age and individually appropriate, respecting the developmental uniqueness of each individual child.

Overplacement: The assignment of a child to the wrong grade. A child who is mismatched with a grade is placed at risk for school failure.

Red-shirting: Holding a child back a year (usually eighth grade) to ensure physical growth and maturity to excel in sports programs.

Re-placement: Allowing a child two years to complete a grade. This intervention is usually in response to a child's need for additional time to complete a program.

Tracking: The practice of grouping children of similar ability level; i.e. high, middle, and low achievers. Tracking is usually long term. Two criticisms: Once a child is placed in a low group, it is difficult to move up. Going through school in the low track can be detrimental to a child's self-concept.

Transition Program: A change in the traditional graded school structure by adding an extra year program before or after kindergarten. This alternative program is for children who are younger in total development. Sometimes called pre-first, pre-kindergarten, bridge class, junior first, or readiness program.

References

CHAPTER 3

Jane M. Healy, Ph.D., Your Child's Growing Mind (New York: Doubleday & Company, Inc., 1987).

CHAPTER 4

Gregg B. Jackson, "The Research Evidence On The Effects Of Grade Retention," Review Of Educational Research, Vol. 45, No. 4, Fall 1975.

Sally L. Smith, No Easy Answers: The Learning Disabled Child, (New York: Bantam Books, 1978).

Louise Bates Ames, Ph.D., Questions Parents Ask: Straight Answers From louise Bates Ames, Ph.D., Associate Director Of The Gesell Institute Of Child Development (New York: Crown Publishers, Inc., 1988).

Leo Galland, Superimmunity For Kids (New York: Doubleday & Company, Inc., 1989).

Stanley K. Turecki & Leslie Tonner, The Difficult Child: A Guide For Parents (New York: Bantam Books, 1985).

CHAPTER 5

H.J. Finlayson, "Nonpromotion And Self-Concept Development," Phi Delta Kappan 59, 3, 1977.

Martin L. Seldman, Performance Without Pressure (New York: Walker & Company, 1988).

Arthur R. Jensen, "Understanding Readiness: An Occasional Paper," (Urbana, Illinois: ERIC Clearinghouse On Elementary And Early Childhood Education, 1969).

Jane M. Healy, Ph.D., Your Child's Growing Mind (New York: Doubleday & Company, Inc., 1987). Paul MacLean p14.

CHAPTER 6

Gerald A. Jennings, Jacqueline Lohraff And Jane Rizzo, "Retention: A Positive Alternative," Teaching K-8, February, 1988.

James K. Uphoff And June E. Gilmore, Summer Children: Ready Or Not For School (Middletown, Ohio: J & J Publishing Company, 1986).

Barbara Carll And Nancy Richard, One Piece Of The Puzzle: A School Readiness Manual (Rosemont, New Jersey: Programs For Education).

CHAPTER 7

Priscilla L. Vail, Smart Kids With School Problems (New York: E.P. Dutton, 1987).

Raymond And Dorothy Moore, Home Spun Kids (Waco, Texas, Word Book Publisher, 1981).

CHAPTER 8

Anthony D. Fredericks, "Retention: Keeping Parents Informed," Teaching K-8, February, 1988.

CHAPTER 9

Carl Tucker III, "Guest Column," School Success Network, Winter, 1988.

Elisabeth Kubler-Ross, On Death And Dying (New York: Macmillan Publisher, 1969).

Linda D. Pass, Taking A Test: The Inside Story (Rosemont, New Jersey: Programs For Education, 1985).

Priscilla L. Vail, "From Gage To Gauge," School Success Network, Winter, 1988.

CHAPTER 10

H. Kaczkowski And C.H. Patterson, Counseling And Psychology In Elementary Schools (Springfield, Illinois: Charles C. Thomas, 1975) p. 306.

Louise Bates Ames, Ph.D., What Am I Doing In This Grade (Rosemont, New Jersey: Programs For Education, 1985).

Janice Hobby, Staying Back (Florida: Triad Publishing, 1982).

Barbara Davis, Getting Another Chance, Montgomery County Maryland

Waldo Jones, School Success Network, Winter, 1988.

Index

About The Author

Jim Grant, a nationally known consultant, was for many years the Teaching Principal at the Temple Elementary School in New Hampshire. He is a charismatic personality who is frequently sought after to speak on the subject of developmental education. He has worked with parents and educators from coast to coast, helping with the introduction and implementation of programs that address school readiness and developmentally appropriate education for young children.

Jim did his undergraduate work at Keene State College and his graduate work at Antioch. In 1982, Franklin Pierce College in Rindge, New Hampshire, conferred an Honorary Doctorate of Humane Letters on him. Father of two, Jim also serves his community as a volunteer fireman, ambulance attendant, and welfare chairman of the Salvation Army.

His down-to-earth style of presenting, coupled with a keen sense of humor, has helped thousands of parents embrace the developmental point of view that children develop at different rates, and a child's developmental level impacts greatly on his or her placement and school success.